iMovie® '09 + iDVD®
FOR
DUMMIES®

I0406546

The iMovie Workspace

Show Camera Import window

Full Screen

Project Library pane

Arrow tool (Advanced only)

Narration

Play Project
from Beginning

Mark as Favorite

Show Inspector

New Project

Swap Projects
and
Events panes

Mark as
Rejected

Audio Skimming On/Off

Viewer

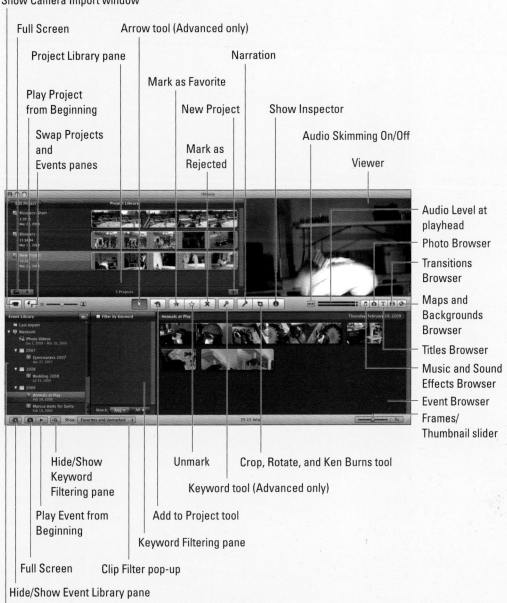

Audio Level at
playhead

Photo Browser

Transitions
Browser

Maps and
Backgrounds
Browser

Titles Browser

Music and Sound
Effects Browser

Event Browser

Frames/
Thumbnail slider

Hide/Show
Keyword
Filtering pane

Unmark

Crop, Rotate, and Ken Burns tool

Keyword tool (Advanced only)

Play Event from
Beginning

Add to Project tool

Keyword Filtering pane

Full Screen

Clip Filter pop-up

Hide/Show Event Library pane

Event Library pane

For Dummies: Bestselling Book Series for Beginners

iMovie® '09 + iDVD® '09 FOR DUMMIES®

Cheat Sheet

The iDVD Workspace

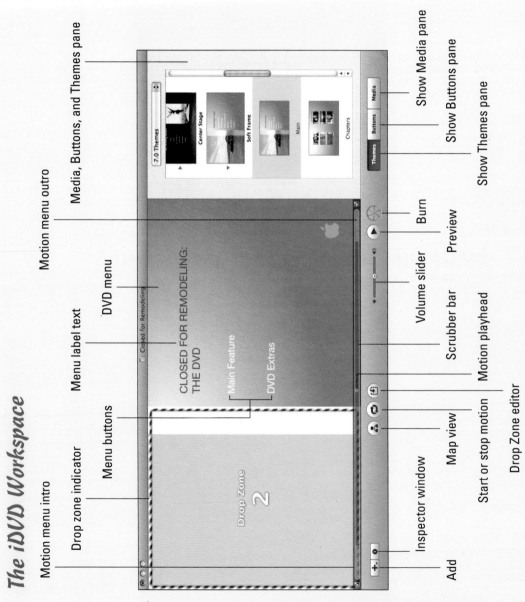

Motion menu intro

Drop zone indicator

Menu buttons

Menu label text

DVD menu

Motion menu outro

Media, Buttons, and Themes pane

Main Feature

DVD Extras

CLOSED FOR REMODELING: THE DVD

Closed for Remodeling

Drop Zone 2

7.0 Themes

Center Stage

Soft Frame

Main

Chapters

Themes

Buttons

Media

Show Media pane

Show Buttons pane

Show Themes pane

Burn

Preview

Volume slider

Scrubber bar

Motion playhead

Drop Zone editor

Inspector window

Map view

Start or stop motion

Add

Wiley, the Wiley Publishing logo, For Dummies, the Dummies Man logo, the For Dummies Bestselling Book Series logo and all related trade dress are trademarks or registered trademarks of John Wiley & Sons, Inc. and/or its affiliates. All other trademarks are property of their respective owners.

Copyright © 2009 Wiley Publishing, Inc. All rights reserved.
Item 0212-9.
For more information about Wiley Publishing, call 1-877-762-2974.

For Dummies: Bestselling Book Series for Beginners

iMovie® '09 & iDVD® '09

FOR

DUMMIES®

by Dennis Cohen and Michael Cohen

WILEY

Wiley Publishing, Inc.

iMovie® '09 & iDVD® '09 For Dummies®

Published by
Wiley Publishing, Inc.
111 River Street
Hoboken, NJ 07030-5774

www.wiley.com

Copyright © 2009 by Wiley Publishing, Inc., Indianapolis, Indiana

Published by Wiley Publishing, Inc., Indianapolis, Indiana

Published simultaneously in Canada

No part of this publication may be reproduced, stored in a retrieval system or transmitted in any form or by any means, electronic, mechanical, photocopying, recording, scanning or otherwise, except as permitted under Sections 107 or 108 of the 1976 United States Copyright Act, without either the prior written permission of the Publisher, or authorization through payment of the appropriate per-copy fee to the Copyright Clearance Center, 222 Rosewood Drive, Danvers, MA 01923, (978) 750-8400, fax (978) 646-8600. Requests to the Publisher for permission should be addressed to the Permissions Department, John Wiley & Sons, Inc., 111 River Street, Hoboken, NJ 07030, (201) 748-6011, fax (201) 748-6008, or online at http://www.wiley.com/go/permissions.

Trademarks: Wiley, the Wiley Publishing logo, For Dummies, the Dummies Man logo, A Reference for the Rest of Us!, The Dummies Way, Dummies Daily, The Fun and Easy Way, Dummies.com, Making Everything Easier, and related trade dress are trademarks or registered trademarks of John Wiley & Sons, Inc. and/or its affiliates in the United States and other countries, and may not be used without written permission. iMovie and iDVD are registered trademarks of Apple, Inc. All other trademarks are the property of their respective owners. Wiley Publishing, Inc., is not associated with any product or vendor mentioned in this book.

LIMIT OF LIABILITY/DISCLAIMER OF WARRANTY: THE PUBLISHER AND THE AUTHOR MAKE NO REPRESENTATIONS OR WARRANTIES WITH RESPECT TO THE ACCURACY OR COMPLETENESS OF THE CONTENTS OF THIS WORK AND SPECIFICALLY DISCLAIM ALL WARRANTIES, INCLUDING WITHOUT LIMITATION WARRANTIES OF FITNESS FOR A PARTICULAR PURPOSE. NO WARRANTY MAY BE CREATED OR EXTENDED BY SALES OR PROMOTIONAL MATERIALS. THE ADVICE AND STRATEGIES CONTAINED HEREIN MAY NOT BE SUITABLE FOR EVERY SITUATION. THIS WORK IS SOLD WITH THE UNDERSTANDING THAT THE PUBLISHER IS NOT ENGAGED IN RENDERING LEGAL, ACCOUNTING, OR OTHER PROFESSIONAL SERVICES. IF PROFESSIONAL ASSISTANCE IS REQUIRED, THE SERVICES OF A COMPETENT PROFESSIONAL PERSON SHOULD BE SOUGHT. NEITHER THE PUBLISHER NOR THE AUTHOR SHALL BE LIABLE FOR DAMAGES ARISING HEREFROM. THE FACT THAT AN ORGANIZATION OR WEBSITE IS REFERRED TO IN THIS WORK AS A CITATION AND/OR A POTENTIAL SOURCE OF FURTHER INFORMATION DOES NOT MEAN THAT THE AUTHOR OR THE PUBLISHER ENDORSES THE INFORMATION THE ORGANIZATION OR WEBSITE MAY PROVIDE OR RECOMMENDATIONS IT MAY MAKE. FURTHER, READERS SHOULD BE AWARE THAT INTERNET WEBSITES LISTED IN THIS WORK MAY HAVE CHANGED OR DISAPPEARED BETWEEN WHEN THIS WORK WAS WRITTEN AND WHEN IT IS READ.

For general information on our other products and services, please contact our Customer Care Department within the U.S. at 877-762-2974, outside the U.S. at 317-572-3993, or fax 317-572-4002.

For technical support, please visit www.wiley.com/techsupport.

Wiley also publishes its books in a variety of electronic formats. Some content that appears in print may not be available in electronic books.

Library of Congress Control Number: TK

ISBN: 978-0-470-50212-9

Manufactured in the United States of America

10 9 8 7 6 5 4 3 2 1

WILEY

About the Authors

Dennis Cohen has been developing software for, and writing about, Macs and related topics for the past quarter-century after an early career writing software at the Jet Propulsion Laboratory for the Deep Space Network. A few of his previous titles are *iLife Bible*; *iTunes, iPhoto, iMovie, and iDVD Bible*; *Teach Yourself Visually iLife '04* and *The Mac Xcode 2 Book* (both with Michael Cohen); and multiple editions of the *FileMaker Pro Bible*. He and Kathy live in Spokane, Washington, providing a home for Kathy's mom, their two dogs, and four cats.

Michael Cohen has been a teacher, an editor, a programmer, a writer, and a multimedia developer. In addition to his collaborations with Dennis, he is the author of *AirPort & Mac Wireless Networks For Dummies*, and *Take Control of Syncing Data in Leopard*, among other titles.

Dedication

This book is dedicated to my lovely wife, Kathy, and the children and grandchildren whom she brought into my life. And, as always, to my constant canine companion, Spenser.

— Dennis Cohen

For Francine Stockser, who wanted to read it.

— Michael Cohen

Authors' Acknowledgments

I would like to thank Apple for providing me with yet another reason to be glad that I use Macs. iLife '09 makes my life easier because it's so easy to use and works so well that I get far fewer tech support calls from family and friends than I used to. Additional thanks go to our editors on this title — Kyle Looper, Linda Morris, and Greg Willmore — and our agent, Carole Jelen, for lining up this gig.

— Dennis Cohen

I second Dennis's thanks to Apple, Kyle, Linda, Greg, and Carole, and offer additional thanks to Bruce Kijewski for a timely hardware assist.

— Michael Cohen

Publisher's Acknowledgments

We're proud of this book; please send us your comments through our online registration form located at http://dummies.custhelp.com. For other comments, please contact our Customer Care Department within the U.S. at 877-762-2974, outside the U.S. at 317-572-3993, or fax 317-572-4002.

Some of the people who helped bring this book to market include the following:

Acquisitions, Editorial

Project Editor: Linda Morris

Acquisitions Editor: Kyle Looper

Copy Editor: Linda Morris

Technical Editor: Greg Willmore

Editorial Manager: Jodi Jensen

Editorial Assistant: Amanda Foxworth

Sr. Editorial Assistant: Cherie Case

Cartoons: Rich Tennant (www.the5thwave.com)

Composition Services

Project Coordinator: Patrick Redmond

Layout and Graphics: Ana Carrillo, Reuben W. Davis, Ronald Terry

Proofreaders: John Greenough, Leeann Harney

Indexer: Broccoli Information Mgt.

Publishing and Editorial for Technology Dummies

  Richard Swadley, Vice President and Executive Group Publisher

  Andy Cummings, Vice President and Publisher

  Mary Bednarek, Executive Acquisitions Director

  Mary C. Corder, Editorial Director

Publishing for Consumer Dummies

  Diane Graves Steele, Vice President and Publisher

Composition Services

  Debbie Stailey, Director of Composition Services

Contents at a Glance

Table of Contents

Part III: In the Cutting Room 109

Chapter 9: Adding Titles, Transitions, and Effects................111

Chapter 10: Precision Editing...................................... 129

Chapter 11: Editing Audio 145

Part IV: Production and Distribution 153

Chapter 12: Sharing Your Movie 155

Introduction

*A*pple pioneered so many things we now take for granted in personal computing. Among these innovations are the menu-driven, graphical user interface (yes, we know they didn't invent it, but Apple pioneered it for the masses) and the digital video application genre. The latter, implemented as iMovie and iDVD, are the subjects of this tome.

For those of you who are used to versions of iMovie prior to iMovie '08, iMovie '09 is going to be a new experience for you. iMovie '08 was all-new from the ground up and iMovie '09 builds on that by adding a lot of new functionality.

iMovie and iDVD are just two of the five applications that comprise the iLife application suite as shipped. (iTunes is considered a part of iLife, but is a free download and not included on the DVD.) The other applications are iPhoto, GarageBand, and iWeb. Although more people probably work with iPhoto than iMovie or iDVD, we think that digital video is the most fun, and iMovie and iDVD empower you to have that fun.

About This Book

First things first, even though this book has *For Dummies* in its title, we don't think of you as dummies. After all, you were intelligent enough to want to learn about iMovie and iDVD, and you came to us to help you find what you seek. We think that's pretty darn smart! The rationale for the *For Dummies* line of books is to present a comfortable environment for you to find out about subjects that interest you but about which you may not know much at the outset.

Apple doesn't provide a manual for the applications in their iLife suite. In fact, the closest thing to documentation in the package is a terse pamphlet that is more advertising than guidance. Apple does offer the obligatory collection of online Help, however, and it covers various aspects of iMovie and iDVD quite well, but you have to know what questions to ask and how to ask them if you want to find the right information. Further, Apple hasn't answered a lot of the questions about these applications that we get asked all the time. Therefore, we've built this book around the things you need to know and answers to the questions we hear people ask.

Conventions Used in This Book

We make frequent use of bullet lists, numbered steps, and screenshots to facilitate your learning because experience has taught us that step-by-step instructions help and that pictures are often worth at *least* a thousand words.

Web addresses (URLs) are presented in a special monospace font (for example, www.apple.com). Menu selections appear like this: File⇨Import⇨iMovie HD Project. This tells you to select the File menu, and then, from the submenu that appears, choose Import, and then finally to select iMovie HD Project from the next submenu that appears.

Icons Used in This Book

Various paragraphs are set off with special icons, as follows:

Advice or information that should help you work more efficiently.

Cautionary information to help you avoid pitfalls.

Somewhat nerdy information that you don't really have to know, but that is either interesting background or helpful to your understanding.

Information that you should really keep in mind because it comes up often.

How This Book Is Organized

Unlike a novel or a textbook where each chapter builds on that which came before, this book is quite a bit less linear in its approach. You can skip around, completely avoiding sections that don't apply to what you're trying to do. For example, if you're assembling pre-existing footage to make a movie, you won't need to know how to import from a camcorder, and if you aren't using high-definition (1080i) content, you can skip sections describing how to work with 1080i material. If, at some later date, you undertake a project that requires 1080i, just go back and peruse the information at that time.

Although you can skip around, a front-to-back reading might be appropriate for traditionalists or for those who just want to make sure that they get all the info that they can. Because some of you crave that start-to-finish coverage, we organized the book to facilitate the linear approach as well, grouping similar subjects as follows.

Part I: Pre-Production and Getting Started

In these early chapters, we give you a little history, introduce the iMovie and iDVD workspaces, provide advice on how to prepare for shooting a movie, and show you how to get your footage into iMovie, manage the iMovie Event Library and Events, and work with clips.

Part II: Doing a Rough Cut

This is where we really get down to the business of iMovie — creating projects, manipulating clips, working with still images, and working with iMovie Themes.

Part III: In the Cutting Room

In these chapters, we cover how to enhance your video; add titles, transitions and effects; perform precision editing such as combining separate audio and video tracks; work with audio; and add chapter markers for use in iDVD.

Part IV: Production and Distribution

In this Part, we cover how to share your video product with others, either through Web sites such as YouTube or MobileMe, or via DVD. In the last four chapters of this Part, we tell you more than you probably want to know about how to design and create DVDs with iDVD.

Part V: The Part of Tens

The two chapters in this part are a *For Dummies* tradition. We introduce ten software and hardware products that can enhance your digital video experience and provide ten tips for troubleshooting common problems.

Where to Go from Here

We think that Chapter 1 is a good place for just about everyone to start. After that, follow along until you hit a topic that isn't germane to your intended use, at which point you can either continue for the sake of completeness or skip to the next relevant heading. Alternatively, if you like the jump cut approach, just skip around to topics of interest.

Because we want to make this book as useful as possible, please let us know what you think we did well or where you would like to see additional information. We might not be able to incorporate all suggestions in future editions (we have book length constraints, after all), but we like to deal with what we can in print or, where appropriate, follow up on the Web.

Part I

Pre-Production and Getting Started

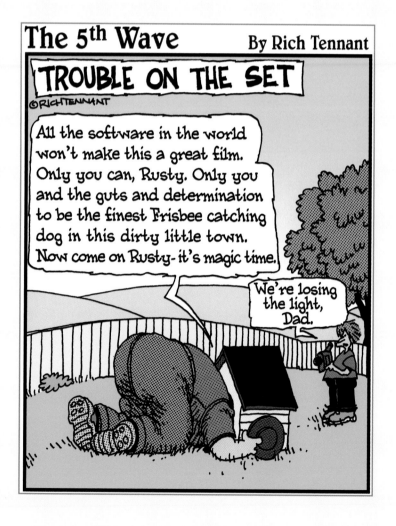

© iStockphoto/Michael Kurtz

In this part . . .

In these four chapters, we cover the following topics:

- ✔ Chapter 1 introduces you to the user interface you encounter when you start using iMovie and iDVD and the basics of how the programs work. It also gives you some history, telling how the programs reached their current forms.

- ✔ Chapter 2 provides guidance on how to plan your movie and how to shoot the best footage you can. It then walks you through getting your video into iMovie.

- ✔ Chapter 3 explores using iMovie's Event Library for organizing your video clips and working with Events.

- ✔ Chapter 4 introduces iMovie tools that help you sort through your Event Library, mark the footage you want to use, and eliminate video segments that just don't measure up to your standards.

1

Making and Sharing Movies

*i*Movie and iDVD, parts of the iLife '09 suite (which includes iTunes, iPhoto, iMovie, iDVD, GarageBand, and iWeb), form the digital video spoke of Apple's so-called "Digital Hub." iLife is bundled with new Macintosh computers and available separately for a $79 list price. iDVD is unchanged from the very mature version shipped in iLife '08 (other than a couple of minor updates). iMovie, on the other hand, has dozens of new features, a few of which are the new Precision Editor; chapter, comment, and beat markers; and themes.

This chapter details the steps along the way that brought iMovie and iDVD to their current incarnations. You also get a brief tour of the iMovie and iDVD Workspaces. Additionally, we cover topics you should keep in mind when planning and creating your movies so that you can achieve the best end result.

© iStockphoto/Kiyoshi Takahase

Getting to iLife '09

In 1999, Apple introduced the iMac DV (Digital Video), the first consumer computer to come with a FireWire port as standard equipment. To demonstrate FireWire's speed and capability, the iMac DV included a new application named iMovie. iMovie was a groundbreaking introduction of home video editing to the masses (or, as Apple prefers to say, "the rest of us"), geared to use the early generation of

MiniDV-tape based camcorders from companies like Sony, Canon, and JVC. All of these companies agreed on FireWire as the standard protocol for transferring video (although it was sometimes called something else, like iLink or IEEE-1394). And iMovie was easy to use, far more so than professional packages like Apple's Final Cut or Adobe's Premiere.

Apple improved and enhanced iMovie through six versions, the last two of which included HD (for High Definition) as part of their name. However, although it was still easier to use than the competition, iMovie gained complexity along with its new capabilities and was still based on code that was originally written for pre-OS X Macs. Then, in late 2007, with the release of iLife '08, a new version of iMovie was introduced. Old-timers like us recognized that the new iMovie made getting started a lot easier and that it fit into the OS X mold more comfortably than its predecessors, but we also noticed that a lot of functionality was either missing or, in a few cases, relocated to GarageBand, the audio editing application in the iLife'09 suite. Apple recognized that many of their existing users would be dissatisfied with the new iMovie, just as new users would be enthused by how easy it was to use, so Apple made iMovieHD available to iLife '08 owners as a free download. The iMovie in iLife '09 is a vast improvement on the previous release and an alternative is no longer necessary nor provided.

Similarly, Apple introduced iDVD at the January 2001 Macworld Expo, providing a tool that enabled purchasers of Macs with the new *SuperDrives* — the first DVD burners priced for the consumer market (from Pioneer) — to produce their own DVDs. The iDVD in iLife '09 is, to all intents and purposes, the same iDVD that shipped as part of iLife '08. The only changes are compatibility updates for the other applications in iLife '09.

Henceforth in this book, we refer to the current software as iLife, iMovie, iDVD, GarageBand, iPhoto, and so on, and include a version number only if we find it necessary to discuss an earlier software iteration.

Knowing What Goes into Making a Movie

Just about any movie that anyone would be willing to watch requires some planning, organization, and editing. Assuming that the content is coming from a camcorder, planning includes being sure to start filming a few seconds before the desired scene to avoid missing the first frame and letting the camera run a few seconds after the end of scene so as not to prematurely end the scene. One of the great things about digital editing in iMovie is how easy it is to trim the footage so that you can start and end each scene with exactly the frames you want.

Of formats and frame rates

Historically there have been, basically, two broadcast standards: NTSC and PAL. Minor variations existed, but NTSC and PAL have been the name of the game outside of France, which still employs a standard called SECAM that was common in Eastern Europe before the fall of the Iron Curtain, when the formerly Communist nations switched to PAL. NTSC is the standard in North and Central America, most South American countries, Japan, the Philippines, and a number of Asian and Pacific Island countries, whereas some variety of PAL is the standard almost everywhere else (except, as mentioned, France). The two major differences between the NTSC and PAL formats are the frame rate — how many frames of video make up a second of footage — and frame size — the number of video scan lines in a frame. NTSC uses 30 fps (frames per second) — really 29.97, but most of the literature rounds this off — and PAL uses 25 fps. Similarly, NTSC has 525 scan lines and PAL has 625, some of which are unused. If you're curious about the nitty-gritty details, the math, and the exceptions, we recommend that you start by searching the Web for more info on NTSC and PAL. While you're Googling, check out some info on ATSC (the format for digital television that supports HDTV) to see how the "digital transition" has simplified many items while introducing its own new technical details to confuse the typical TV viewer.

Organization includes having your camera and microphone, if you have an external microphone, positioned to catch the scene to the best advantage. In other words, your scene needs to be properly lit with the audio pickup where you'll catch and immortalize any dialogue. (We could show you a wedding video where the camcorder was behind the groom by about 15 feet and his vows didn't come through.) In fact, when you can arrange to do so, have multiple cameras recording from different angles. iMovie makes it easy to splice in both audio and video, and having multiple sources not only means that you're far less likely to miss something, but that you can use the best audio while cutting from one camera angle to another to best present your scene. That's why professional videographers use multiple cameras, too. Other organizational items include making sure that you have adequate batteries or available power, sufficient media (be it tape, flash memory, MiniDVDs, or available hard drive space), and satisfactory lighting. And, if your movie is scripted, you need to make sure that everyone knows what they're supposed to do and say as well as where they're supposed to be while giving their performance.

The editing, well, that's just what we're going to cover in subsequent chapters, mostly in Chapters 5 and 6. iMovie lets you do easily almost anything that a professional editor does, without all of the hard work and training.

Understanding the Movie-Making Process

Oversimplifying the subject tremendously, movies fall into one of two categories: documentaries or scripted. Documentaries include not just the polished product of collecting and narrating historic footage, but efforts as unpolished as the traditional home movie, where you just throw the camera up and grab footage of some unplanned event, such as baby's first steps, animals frolicking, or the first time your child succeeds in riding his two-wheeler. Scripted movies range from recording planned scenes such as class lectures to elaborately scripted vehicles that include not only prepared dialogue but elaborate stage direction.

Television tends to blur traditional categorization, referring to the current plethora of "reality" shows as unscripted; however, they fall more into the scripted category than not, with prepared venues and planned activities. The shows lack only the precise details of a traditional scripted show, just as a variety show or a talk show leaves a lot of room for improvisation although it's still a planned show. The stunts or routines in a show like *Survivor* or *Dancing with the Stars* are planned and scripted, but how well they're executed varies, just as the host of a talk show has a prepared list of questions (or script), but doesn't always know how the guest is going to respond.

Just because most home movies are basically documentary, immortalizing events and activities, doesn't mean you can't put a little structure into the process. iMovie (and its companion, iPhoto) help you by grouping footage and images into *events* — content organized initially by time, but customizable by you. We discuss events in more detail in Chapter 3.

Entire books are dedicated to the art and science of film-making. If you're interested, a good starting point is *Filmmaking For Dummies* (Bryan Michael Stoller, Wiley Publishing).

Figuring Out What's Where in iMovie

 The first time you launch iMovie (by clicking its icon in the Dock — a five-pointed star with a circled video camera in the center, as shown in the margin), you encounter a screen that looks like Figure 1-1. Some minor details in the menu bar and Dock may differ depending on your screen size and what software you have installed, but the iMovie window and the Welcome to iMovie dialog will be the same.

Apple realizes that you probably won't want to see the Welcome dialog every time you launch iMovie, so they include a check box in the lower-left corner that you can deselect after you've taken advantage of the information it offers (or decide that you don't want to investigate). You won't see it again unless you choose Help⇨Welcome to iMovie. The tutorials are useful and exhibit the quality and attention to detail that we've come to expect from Apple — we heartily recommend them as an adjunct to this book.

After you've dismissed the Welcome dialog, you're left with iMovie's main window, which Apple refers to as the Workspace (see Figure 1-2). This is the Workspace's default configuration. You can, up to a point, change which panes are shown and in what positions via iMovie's preference settings (iMovie⇨Preferences, or ⌘+, (comma)), items in the View menu, and items in the Window menu. By default, you see the Project Library pane in the upper left, the Viewer pane in the upper right, and the Event Library in the lower half. The Event Library is split into a hierarchical view on the left and a browser view on the right, displaying the clips in any selected event, with a horizontal toolbar in the middle of the Workspace and a control bar for the Event Library along the bottom of the window.

Although we laud Apple's user interface consistency, every once in a while, even they slip up, and we think this is one of those situations. The Project Library has similar controls to the Event Library, and it is clear that the controls "belong" to the Project Library by their appearance. The controls for the Event Library don't match in the same way, appearing as part of the window frame. But, if you click the toolbar button to swap the Project and Events areas, the controls swap appearance as well. It just goes to show you that nobody's perfectly consistent.

Figure 1-1:
Presenting
iMovie.

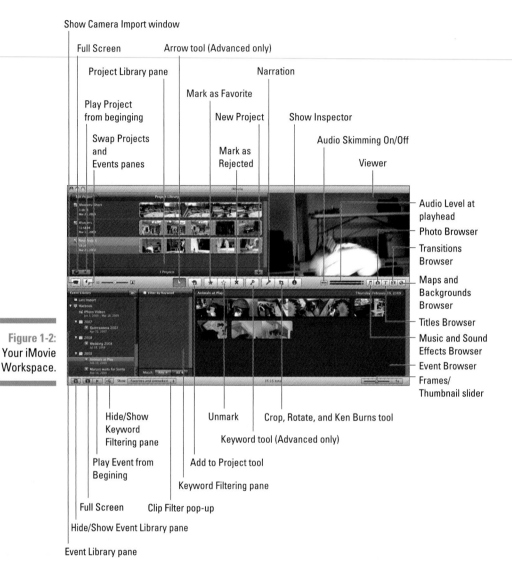

Show Camera Import window

Full Screen

Arrow tool (Advanced only)

Project Library pane

Narration

Mark as Favorite

Play Project
from begining

New Project

Show Inspector

Swap Projects
and
Events panes

Mark as
Rejected

Audio Skimming On/Off

Viewer

Audio Level at
playhead

Photo Browser

Transitions
Browser

Maps and
Backgrounds
Browser

Titles Browser

Music and Sound
Effects Browser

Event Browser

Frames/
Thumbnail slider

Figure 1-2:
Your iMovie
Workspace.

Hide/Show
Keyword
Filtering pane

Unmark

Crop, Rotate, and Ken Burns tool

Keyword tool (Advanced only)

Play Event from
Begining

Add to Project tool

Keyword Filtering pane

Full Screen

Clip Filter pop-up

Hide/Show Event Library pane

Event Library pane

If you have movie clips in your iPhoto Library, iMovie asks you whether you want thumbnails created for use in your Event Library now or whether you wish to wait and perform the processing later, as shown in Figure 1-3. This activity takes place because a lot of still cameras are capable of recording video and iPhoto imports those videos into the iPhoto Library. As we discuss in Chapter 2, iMovie works with content from a variety of sources, including iPhoto.

Figure 1-3:
Now or
later for
iPhoto video
thumbnails?

TIP

In this example, we told iMovie to process the iPhoto videos so that we have some content in our Event Library to illustrate the rest of this discussion. That's why the Event Library sports an iPhoto Videos item in the following screenshots, an item that wasn't present in Figure 1-2.

Exploring the Event Library

As shown in Figure 1-4, we selected iPhoto Videos in the Event Library list on the left and its four clips appear to the right. The number of thumbnails, and thus the apparent clip length, is controlled by the duration slider at the bottom-right of the window — the duration selected determines how many thumbnails are shown. In our example, the duration is set for 5 seconds, so clips shorter than 5 seconds in length are one thumbnail wide, between 5 and 10 seconds are two thumbnails wide, and if we had a longer clip of between 10 and 15 seconds, it would be three wide, and so on. You can modify this granularity by moving the duration slider. When you hover the cursor over a clip, its duration appears at the left, just above an action drop-down menu (the little gear icon with the down-pointing arrowhead to its right), and a red positional indicator line follows your *scrubbing* action (the movement, back and forth, through the clip) while the particular frames play in the Viewer.

Along the control bar at the bottom of the window, the left-most button controls whether the Events list is showing or hidden: if the Events list is present, the little arrowhead points to the left, indicating that you can click to hide the Events list (slide it out of view to the left). If the Events list is hidden, the arrowhead is on the right, indicating that you can bring the Events list back into view. The next button to the right, when clicked, puts you in full-screen mode. The menu bar, Dock, and all your windows disappear, as shown in Figure 1-5. When you first enter full-screen mode, only the viewer area is visible, but if you move your cursor to the bottom of the screen, the controls appear. Pressing the spacebar toggles between playing and pausing whatever is being viewed. You can also play events full-screen by choosing Window⇨Show Events Full-Screen (⌘+7).

Figure 1-4:
The Events
Library with
an event
selected.

Action drop-down menu button

Duration slider

Fullscreen mode

Show/Hide Events list

Figure 1-5:
View your
event video
full-screen.

If you have the controls showing in full-screen mode, you can scrub across the thumbnails to determine what's visible in the viewer. Clicking the circled X at the bottom left of the screen exits full-screen mode, but if you don't want to have to show the controls, you can also exit full-screen mode by pressing Esc.

The Show pop-up menu (refer to Figure 1-4) lets you control which clips are shown in the Event pane: Favorites only, Favorites and Unmarked (⌘+L), All Clips, or Rejected Clips. We cover rejecting clips and marking favorites in Chapter 4.

Deciding on a Distribution Plan

Modern technology has significantly expanded how and where we can share our video products. It wasn't all that long ago that camcorders were bulky things that recorded on VHS, Beta, or VHS-C video cassettes, and distribution was pretty much limited to duplicating tapes and handing or sending out copies. Besides the enormous inconvenience, copying tape was a lossy proposition (meaning quality was lost), both from duplicating analog data and the fact that tape was flexible, stretched with repeated use, and was magnetic, making it susceptible to electromagnetic interference.

DVDs and their predecessors, VideoCDs (VCD) and Super VideoCDs (SVCD), eliminated the generational degradation inherent in the analog copying process by moving to digital technology.

That quality loss is avoided only when you're creating a duplicate, not when you're re-encoding to a different format, a process known as *transcoding*. All standard distribution formats, such as MPEG-1, MPEG-2, MPEG-4, and DivX (or Xvid) employ lossy data compression to keep the size of your video manageable, just as JPEG compresses images and MP3 and AAC compress audio in a manner that throws away some (hopefully) unimportant bits.

In addition to DVDs, we now have iPods, iPhones, Web pages, YouTube, and a myriad of other distribution venues for our content. iMovie, with the help of QuickTime, lets you choose which output format or formats you desire. You can create a movie optimized for iPod viewing, create a copy targeted to Apple TV, and then instruct iMovie to send the content off to iDVD. It's up to you to decide how you want your movies distributed, and we give you a helping hand with the details in Chapter 12 and give extensive coverage to iDVD in Part IV.

Checking Out iDVD

Although we now have many different venues and methods for sharing our videos, we're still particularly partial to the DVD. Almost everyone we know, and certainly everyone we know with whom we want to share content, has a DVD player. Not everyone we know has an Internet connection, particularly the broadband variety that is a virtual necessity for accessing viewable video over the ether. Although Apple didn't enhance iDVD's feature set in iLife '09, they did revise iDVD for compatibility with the other iLife applications and included iDVD as one of the six iLife components. This is apparently an acknowledgement on Apple's part that, although they consider DVD an old technology that is going to be made obsolete by online and high-definition offerings, it is still a dominant distribution venue at this time.

The Select a Task window

When you first launch iDVD, you see the window shown in Figure 1-6. Along the window's bottom, you find a Help button (question mark), a button that launches your Web browser and takes you to Apple's Web site and the page with the iDVD tutorials (Video Tutorials), and a Quit button. The tutorials don't teach you anything that isn't in this book, but they are presented as video, so if watching a video helps you learn, the tutorials are a helpful adjunct to what you're holding.

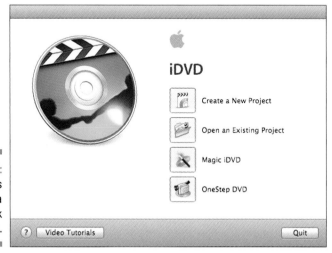

Figure 1-6:
iDVD's
Select a
Task
window.

The Create a New Project button does just what the name suggests. Click it and you're presented with the Create Project dialog shown in Figure 1-7, where you name your project in the Save As text box, specify where the project should be saved in the Where pop-up menu (or click the down-pointing arrow to the right of the Save As text box and navigate in the expanded Save dialog to another location), and click the radio button that tells iDVD whether the project is going to have a 4:3 aspect ratio (Standard) or 16:9 (Widescreen). The Open an Existing Project button also is self-descriptive, presenting you with an Open dialog that enables you to select an existing project with which you wish to work. Use Magic DVD to quickly assemble a DVD from a collection of existing videos and photos — just drag and drop the media into iDVD, and Magic DVD does the rest. OneStep DVD lets you import video directly from your camera or a movie and put it on DVD. OneStep DVD is an excellent way to make a quick DVD of video you don't intend to edit. OneStep DVD and Magic DVD are covered in Chapter 13. Now, we're just going to briefly introduce the iDVD Workspace you see when you create a new project or open an existing project.

Figure 1-7:
Specify your project's name, location, and aspect ratio here.

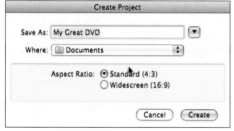

Themes, Buttons, and the Media Browser

When you click Create, the dialog disappears and you'll see a progress dialog while iDVD loads the Themes, and so on, before you arrive at the main project window, shown in Figure 1-8. The leftmost pane displays the menu on which you're currently working — initially, it shows the main menu for the selected Theme. The pane to the right displays available Themes, Buttons, or the Media Browser, depending upon which of the three buttons below the pane you've clicked.

Themes includes a pop-up menu where you choose from which set of themes you want to make your selection: All, those that appeared with iDVD 7, those debuting in iDVD 6, those introduced in iDVD 5, those from older versions of iDVD, or those you specify as Favorites. Themes have the same purpose as templates in a word-processing or graphics program. You select a theme to provide your DVD with a consistent design, employing professionally designed backgrounds, buttons, and other elements.

Figure 1-8:
Introducing
the iDVD
project
window.

Clicking Buttons enables you to specify how you want your menu buttons to appear. Unlike the computer-based menus to which you're accustomed, a DVD menu is a screen with buttons or labels on it. Menu buttons are the visual elements that you navigate and select with your DVD remote control, selecting such things as what to play, whether subtitles are on or off, or whether to play a narration track. Although they're called buttons, as you'll see in the following list, they don't have to look like computer (or physical) buttons at all. Your choices are

- **Text:** Simple text, although you can designate an underlining style that appears when the button is selected
- **Bullets:** Small icons that show up when the button is selected
- **Shapes:** Graphic elements that appear behind the button when selected
- **Frames:** Framing rectangles
- **Artistic:** Fancy borders for your button
- **Rectangle:** Various boxes that surround your button
- **Rounded:** Curved boxes that surround your button

With any of the last four button types, selecting the slashed circle icon from the styles that appear in that category applies a default border to your button, but selecting any other style includes a graphic thumbnail displaying a preview of your content (the default is a 30-second video loop).

Selecting Media allows you to specify content for use on your DVD, either as part of the menu structure or the actual content. You see the Media Browser a lot in this book — it's the interface between the different iLife applications. For example, in iDVD, you would use the Media Browser to select movies created in iMovie, audio created in GarageBand or stored in your iTunes Library, and photos from your iPhoto Library.

2

Creating and Assembling Your Source Material

In This Chapter

▷ Creating your shooting plan

▷ Shooting what you planned

*I*f you don't have a script or a plan and aren't shooting your own video, but are just assembling existing material from other sources, feel free to skip over this chapter. However, if you're planning the next dramatic blockbuster or comedy tour-de-farce (pun intended), or just an organized event that has yet to occur (such as a sporting event, birthday party, or wedding), you can find material here to help you ensure that you don't forget something. In addition, we offer tips for taking better footage. The following discussions cover as many bases as possible, without delving into a complete rehash of *Filmmaking For Dummies* (Bryan Michael Stoller, Wiley Publishing). You might not need to heed all the advice, but you should at least consider each suggestion before dismissing it as overkill for your project.

© iStockphoto

Planning Your Shoot

You might think that planning your shoot just involves giving your actors their scripts, stage directions, and a chance to rehearse, but that's just the tip of the iceberg!

Arranging the venue

Suppose that you're chronicling the nuptials of someone you really wish to please with your effort: Maybe they're paying you, or maybe you're giving them this effort as your wedding gift. The first things you need to consider are where you can set up, whether you can get by with only one camera angle (yeah, right!), where the camera(s) need to be positioned, where the microphone(s) need to be located, how much control you have over the lighting and its position, and whether auxiliary power is available without interfering with the event. (Power cords tripping the ushers, guests, or bridal party are sure to ruin things.)

When it comes to audio, relying on the built-in microphone in your camcorder to collect excellent sound is like counting on a politician to tell the truth, the whole truth, and nothing but the truth. You might get lucky and get good sound if you're close to the action, if ambient noise levels are low, and if your subjects speak clearly and with adequate volume for the microphone to pick them up. But those are a lot of *ifs*. Occasionally, the internal microphone even picks up camera noises (for example, the whirring noise when you zoom in or out). Most camcorders have an attachment for an external microphone and, if it's within your budget, having an external microphone gives you more options when it comes to getting the best audio possible.

At a wedding, we would suggest placing one camera behind the officiant so that you have a good shot of the couple, with an emphasis on the bride, and one behind the couple or the groom, to give you a good shot of the officiant, as a minimum. You should also have at least one microphone positioned between the officiant and the couple to make certain that you catch the invocation and the vows: Your camcorders' microphones can easily miss at least part of the dialogue or record it so faintly that viewers won't be able to make out what was said. One possible safety net is to set up a Mac with GarageBand running and a good microphone attached to catch everything and then dub it back into your movie.

Most microphones come with foam covers. These covers not only protect the microphone from scratches, minor dents, and an accumulation of filth, but filter out wind sounds, as well as reducing various vocal distractions, such as sibilant *s* sounds or the popping of *p* and *b* sounds.

Another thing you can do to preview what your audio will sound like is to plug a set of headphones into the camcorder's headphone jack and listen to what the camcorder is "hearing."

Lighting should ideally be located above, slightly behind, and to the side of (say, at a 30 degree angle) the camera. The closer you can come to this ideal, the better, but you should avoid shooting into the light at all costs. Similarly, you should avoid having the light directly atop the camera, especially if you're going to be getting full-face shots: Red-eye is much harder to fix in video than it is in still photos.

Lining up your resources

It's been said that timing is everything. We don't know if that absolute is true, but timing and scheduling are certainly important factors in successfully making a movie.

If you're lining up the venue and producing a movie with pre-planned scenes and dialogue, here are some of the items you should remember to schedule:

- **The location:** Whether you're working on a traditional sound stage or some other venue, you need to schedule its use, giving yourself enough time for setup as well as shooting time.

- **The cast and crew:** All involved parties need to know when they need to be there, what they need to bring, and what preparatory work they need to do. This can include learning lines, setting up scenery, applying makeup, or getting into costume.

- **The equipment:** Cameras, microphones, props, and so forth need to be available. You might need to rent or borrow some equipment – verify that it is available when needed.

The larger your project, the more involved your scheduling is and the more care you need to put into it. Even a small project should, at a minimum, have a checklist of to-do items. For larger projects, you should consider building a timeline, or even using a project management system to track your dependencies and help you identify conflicts before they throw your schedule out of whack. Lots of project management tools are available. We have used OmniPlan (www.omnigroup.com) and iTaskX (www.itaskx.com) for our projects, but many others are available. Both offer trial versions, so you can easily check out their suitability for your purposes. Figures 2-1 and 2-2 show a couple of sample screens from OmniPlan and Figures 2-3 and 2-4 show the iTaskX screens using the same input data.

Figure 2-1: OmniPlan's Resource Chart.

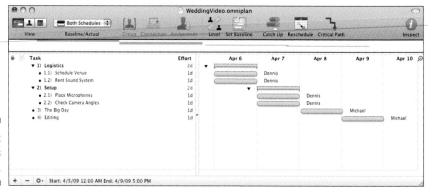

Figure 2-2:
OmniPlan's
Gannt Chart.

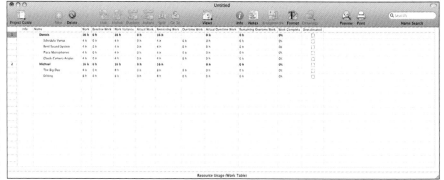

Figure 2-3:
iTaskX's
Resource
Chart.

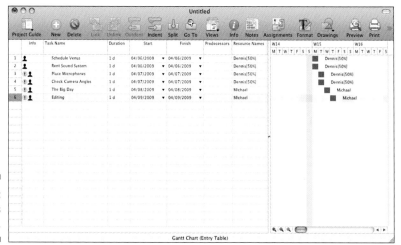

Figure 2-4:
iTaskX's
Gannt Chart.

If you opt for a project management system, please remember that they are only as good as the data they're fed. *GIGO* (garbage-in, garbage-out) is especially true when creating a timeline and dependency chart (they're usually called *Gantt charts*, after Henry Gannt). All the conclusions drawn are tied directly to the input data. If, for example, you tell the program that a given task takes two hours, all subsequent activity scheduling is based on that estimate and all conflict-checking is also based on that estimate. Similarly, if you specify that a particular individual or resource is needed for a task, the dependency checking schedules the task so that it isn't concurrent with any other task requiring that resource. On the other hand, if you forget to include a necessary resource, the scheduler might end up making the task overlap another task that also requires the resource. Many projects go awry because the input data is incomplete, unrealistic or, at the very least, overly optimistic. This applies not only to time, but also to cost. Double- and triple-check to make certain that nothing is omitted and include a little padding to deal with the unexpected — Murphy and his laws are alive, well, and pop in at the most inopportune times.

Shooting Your Plan

The military has an adage: "No battle plan survives the first contact with the enemy." Moviemakers can adapt that philosophy as "No shooting schedule survives past the first scene." The following examples should illustrate why having a "Plan B" (and C and D, and so on) is a necessity.

Be prepared

Okay, you've planned everything, scheduled everything, and are now ready to implement your artistic vision. Now you hear that one of your cast has cracked a tooth and is at the dentist: What is your contingency plan? Are there scenes you can shoot in the current location with the available cast and crew that don't involve the poor soul at the dentist?

Another factor that could affect your schedule is the weather. Did you plan to shoot an outdoor scene only to have the weatherman send you an unexpected rainstorm when you needed a sunlit day?

One of the advantages using a Gannt chart offers is that, based upon your input, you can usually identify tasks you might switch to that aren't dependent upon the missing resource or the capriciousness of Zeus.

Alternatively, now that you've started shooting, you're finding that your cast doesn't have their parts down quite well enough or that they're a little distracted, presenting you with great fodder for a "blooper reel," but not getting the scene you want. Meanwhile, your camera battery is running low. Did you remember to bring spare, fully charged batteries, or do you have a convenient electric outlet so you can run off AC power? You're also running low on tape or whatever other media you might be using (such as mini-DVD/RWs). Hopefully, you remembered to always keep spare media available. Of course, if you're using a camcorder that records to a hard drive or flash memory, it's easy enough to just erase the bad takes and re-record, but then you risk losing what might be some really good blooper material.

If you don't have multiple cameras available, try to tape more than one take of a scene, possibly from a slightly different angle. This gives you a fallback position in case you later discover something slightly awry, and it might allow you to do a cut from one camera angle to another in order to improve your presentation.

When filming an unscripted event, such as a school play, you're quite likely to encounter other doting parents and grandparents recording the same event. Ask around to see if you can "pool" footage and get that more professional, multiple camera look.

Although it seems trite and harkens back to the movies of the 1930s and 1940s about making films, recording a clapboard or even just a sign with information about the scene you're preparing to shoot provides two important elements: identifying the scene and guaranteeing that the camera is rolling before the real action begins. If you're a traditionalist (or just a little silly), you can even call out, "Lights, camera, action . . . scene two, take two," or something similar. All of the work involved shouldn't detract from the joy making a movie can offer.

When pooling footage or using multiple cameras, try as hard as you can to match input formats. For example, if you're filming in HD, try to find others who are also using an HD camcorder (or at least a widescreen aspect ratio). The closer you can match input formats, the better (or at least more consistent) the output will be.

Getting the best footage you can

Basically, three common errors ruin most amateur film efforts: bouncing, jittery camera work; poorly lit scenes; and bad audio. You can avoid these pitfalls, in most cases, by heeding the advice in the following sections.

Avoiding the jitters

Most modern digital camcorders (other than the really inexpensive ones) include some stabilization circuitry. The provided stabilization takes care of really minor shaking, but doesn't help when it comes to the bouncy video resulting from moving the camera around, especially across an uneven surface. iMovie also provides some new stabilization routines that help to smooth out jittery video, but the software can only do so much. Avoiding the problem in the first place means that you don't have to rely on how much the camera or iMovie's routines can do to fix the problem. Your best bet to inexpensively avoid bouncing images is a tripod.

If you have more money in the budget, you might even consider a Steadicam or other gyro-balanced camera mount. Lacking the budget, improvise by using a table, fence rail, or car/truck hood as your temporary tripod. Pan slowly — it not only reduces jitter, but also doesn't give your audience visual whiplash.

Zooming in and out rapidly can give your viewers a queasy feeling. Slow, smooth zooming, when zooming is called for at all, is the ticket. And avoid digital zoom: Digital zoom is merely a magnification and interpolation in your camera's software, resulting in generally blocky and unrealistic-looking footage (unless that is the effect you're seeking). If you need more zoom than offered by your camera's optical zoom, you should really find a way to get closer. Figure 2-5 shows a frame where digital zooming was (ab)used.

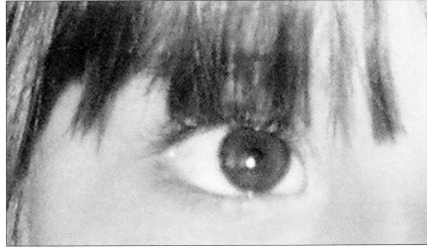

Figure 2-5:
Digital
zooming can
make your
footage look
fake.

Letting in the light

Your camcorder is an electronic device and doesn't see light the same way your eye sees light. In low-light conditions, your eye automatically dilates to let in more light, and this can lead you to believe that there's enough light for the scene. Unless you manually adjust your camera, it is unlikely to agree with you. Find out what lighting settings your camera allows and set them appropriately for the prevailing conditions. Most camcorders have settings for low-light and low-contrast situations, as well as a *white-balance* adjustment used to eliminate color casts.

Different types of light sources cast a different tint onto the light they provide. The human eye filters out these color casts before we even recognize their presence. A camera actually records what is present. Sunlight tends toward blue, incandescent lights (you know, the ones we're replacing with the compact fluorescent lights that look like spirals) tend toward a yellow tinge, and fluorescent lights gravitate toward green. Use your camera's white balance adjustment to accommodate the lighting for the scene you're about to shoot.

Every decent camcorder includes a menu of pre-programmed adjustments for different lighting conditions. The downside is that every manufacturer uses different names for these adjustments and camera manuals are frequently poorly written (or at least poorly translated into English). Fortunately, though, the sections on the adjustments are almost always short and comprehensible, other than the possibly tortured English. Take the time to learn what your camera has to offer you.

Getting clean audio

We can't overemphasize the importance of checking that you're capturing the audio properly. Wearing headphones, as mentioned earlier in this chapter, is an excellent way to verify that the camera is capturing what it should and not recording undesired audio. If possible, having additional audio sources so that you can dub in as needed in post-production is great insurance.

Even a simple clip-on microphone generally provides better audio fidelity than your camera's mic, especially if you aren't filming a close-up. Microphones fall into four basic categories:

- **Cardioid:** The heart-shaped pickup region gives this category its name. Cardioid microphones, although directed mostly forward, also pick up audio from the sides and rear. These microphones, when used in the camera, pick up various camera sounds (such as the tape transport mechanism or the zoom motor) in addition to the background noises you might want.

- **Directional:** The traditional example of a directional microphone is the shotgun microphone. Its narrow, elliptical pickup region focuses on what is in front of the camera and picks up very little audio from the sides and virtually none from behind the microphone.

✓ **Super-cardioid:** The super-cardioid microphone is the one most commonly found on camcorders. It is essentially a compromise between the cardioid and directional microphone, with an elliptical pickup region that isn't as narrow as the directional.

✓ **Omnidirectional:** These microphones pick up sound from all directions equally well, as the name indicates. Most clip-on and lavaliere microphones, like newscasters wear, are omnidirectional.

If you know that your subjects are going to be relatively stationary, you might consider employing a boom microphone. You can fashion one out of a super-cardioid microphone hanging from a wire above the scene, just outside the camera's view.

Importing Your Video

After you've gotten your ducks in a row and you have lots of video with which to work, you need to get it into iMovie. iMovie accepts video from numerous sources, although the most common is a camcorder. Other common contributors include your Mac's iSight camera (if it has one), camera video clips that are in your iPhoto Library, and video clips you have on your hard drive or other storage media.

Getting video from your camcorder

iMovie works with both FireWire camcorders, which are tape-based, and USB 2.0 camcorders, which are commonly hard-drive, flash, or DVD-RW based. (*FireWire* and *USB2* are different types of cable used to connect your camcorder to your computer.) Other than the obvious difference in the type of connection required, a significant difference is that tape-based camcorders are sequential access devices, meaning that you have to advance or rewind through the content until you've positioned the camera to a specific clip and then have to monitor the import process to bring in desired clip or clips. The USB-based devices are random access, meaning that you can (virtually) instantaneously access any clip just as if it were a file on a hard disk or CD or DVD — because, to all intents, that's just what it is.

As a result of this fundamental difference in how you access content, the interfaces for importing from these different camera types are somewhat different.

Importing from a FireWire camera

The original standard for use with iMovie, FireWire-based mini-DV camcorders provide both a number of advantages and disadvantages compared with the USB camcorders we discuss shortly. Among the advantages are

- The (essentially) uncompressed DV video stream is of relatively high quality.
- The tape to archive your footage is relatively inexpensive (about $2-$3/hour tape, currently) if you need or want to access it in the future.
- FireWire provides *device control*, meaning that your Mac (and iMovie) can control the camera when they're connected, having it play, rewind, fast-forward, and so forth.
- You can share your tapes between multiple cameras.

The disadvantages, however, are

- DV streams take up about 200MB/minute (12GB/hour).
- They are sequential access (requiring frequent fast-forwarding and rewinding to locate footage you seek).
- Data transfer is slower because you have to play the tape to make the transfer.

When you connect a tape-based camera, iMovie presents a window similar to that shown in Figure 2-6.

When you click the Import button (in the lower right of the screen) with the Automatic toggle set (lower-left), iMovie prompts you with the dialog shown in Figure 2-7. Choose the *volume* (a techie name that usually means the same thing as *disk*) to which you want to save your clips using the Save To pop-up menu. The Add to Existing Event and Create New Event radio buttons are pretty much self-explanatory: Because there are no existing Events in our brand-new Event Library, the Add to Existing Event item and its related pop-up menu are disabled. If you want all the footage to go to one event, deselect (uncheck) the Split days into new Events check box; otherwise, iMovie splits the content into new events for each taping date. If you want iMovie to employ its stabilization routines on the clips, select the Analyze for Stabilization After Import check box. Don't worry: If you don't stabilize at this point, you can always select the clip and stabilize it later. After you've set your import options, click Import and iMovie instructs your camera to rewind the tape to the beginning and then start importing, showing your progress in hours, minutes, and seconds.

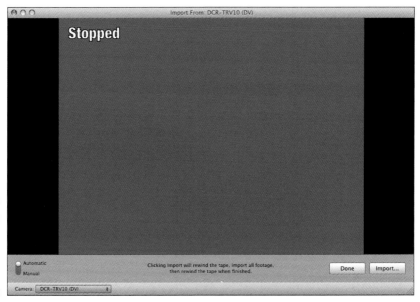

Stopped

Figure 2-6:
Ready to
import from
a FireWire
camera.

Figure 2-7:
Setting your
options for
iMovie to
auto-import
your tape.

Even with the toggle set to Automatic, you can still halt the import process by clicking the Stop button.

When the import is complete, iMovie presents the process dialog shown at the top of Figure 2-8 while generating thumbnails for the imported clips. After generating the thumbnails, iMovie tells you about how much video it imported (bottom of Figure 2-8).

Generating Thumbnails

Processing Event: New Event 2–19–09

Time remaining: about 3 minutes

Figure 2-8:
iMovie
generates
thumbnails
for imported
clips.

Camera Import Complete

About 10 minutes of video were imported.

OK

Figure 2-8:
iMovie
generates
thumbnails
for imported
clips.

If you want to import selected clips rather than everything on the tape, flip the toggle from Automatic to Manual and watch the import window for your camera sprout a few extra controls, as shown in Figure 2-9. The added buttons, from left to right, are Rewind, Fast-Forward, Stop, and Play/Pause (if paused or stopped, the arrow for Play shows; if playing, Pause's double vertical bar symbol shows). Use these buttons to control your camera and position to the footage you want to import. When you're ready, click the Import button. The same process as for Automatic import now unfolds, except that you don't receive a message telling you how much video you imported.

When you are finished importing (for the time being), click the Done button to return to iMovie's workspace and notice that your newly imported clips are now in the Event Library, as indicated in Figure 2-10.

Import From: DCR-TRV10 (DV)

00:00:00

Automatic
Manual

00:00:00

Done   Import...

Camera: DCR-TRV10 (DV)

Figure 2-9:
Manual
import
provides
controls
for you to
locate the
particular
clips you
want.

Figure 2-10:
The import
is complete
and your
video is in
the Event
Library.

Importing from a USB recorder

Connecting your USB camera presents a slightly different interface, as shown
in Figure 2-11 for Manual mode. The bottom half of the window displays
thumbnails for each clip on your camera's media (hard drive, flash, or
mini-DVD), each with a check mark below indicating that it is to be imported.
The check boxes and the Uncheck All button are absent in Automatic mode,
where import is all or nothing. If, in Manual mode, you uncheck any of the
clips, the Import All button changes to read Import Checked.

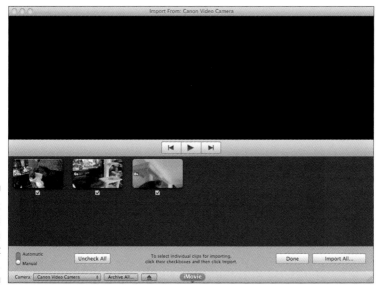

Figure 2-11:
A USB
camcorder's
Import
window.

At the bottom of the Import window is a button labeled Archive All. We can't emphasize strongly enough how valuable backups are, and this button is your gateway to archiving the clips residing on your camera's media, allowing you to erase and reuse the space for new footage while still having the clips for future use and reference. Click Archive All and iMovie presents a collapsed Save dialog, as shown at the left in Figure 2-12, where you can name the archive, if you don't like the default name, and choose a location from the Where pop-up menu. Click the blue button with the triangle to the right of the Save As text box to expand the Save dialog as shown in Figure 2-12 on the right. Personally, we prefer the added flexibility of the expanded dialog, with its familiar Finder-like interface. You can choose File⇨Import⇨From Archive to import archived clips at a later time or to a different account's iMovie Event Library.

Next appears the Import dialog shown in Figure 2-13, asking where you want to save the clips, whether you want to create a new Event or add to an existing Event (and, if so, which one), whether to create new Events if the clip was shot on a different day, and whether to perform image stabilization after the import. It also gives you a chance to specify (again) a setting for 1080i high-definition video.

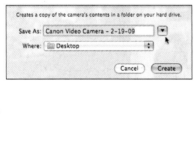

Figure 2-12:
Save an
archive
of your
camera's
contents
(L:collapsed,
R: expanded).

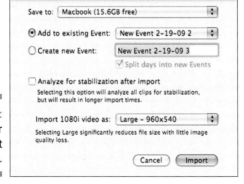

Figure 2-13:
Set your
import
options.

Click Import All (or Import Checked) and iMovie starts the import, indicating below each thumbnail where in the process it is, as shown in Figure 2-14. When complete, iMovie presents a dialog informing you how many clips and how much total time they represent were imported.

When you're finished importing, click the Done button to dismiss the Import From window. The new Event or Events are displayed in the Event Library, as shown in Figure 2-15.

Figure 2-14: Import in progress.

Figure 2-15: Your new Event appears in the Event Library.

Please be sure to unmount your camera before disconnecting it from the computer. The Eject button at the bottom of the Import From window is the easiest method, but you can also open a Finder window and click the Eject button next to your camera's entry in the Finder window's sidebar. If you disconnect your camera without unmounting it first, you risk damage to the media (slight) or to the content on that media.

Recording video from your iSight camera

Many Macs (the MacBook, MacBook Pro, MacBook Air, and iMac) come with iSight cameras built in. Although Apple no longer manufactures or sells them, you can still find external FireWire iSight cameras available on eBay and other such sites. These are excellent adjuncts to Mac minis and MacPros that don't include the camera. You can invoke the Import From window by clicking the Camera icon or choosing File⇨Import from Camera (⌘+I). If no other cameras are connected, the Import From window defaults to the iSight, as shown in Figure 2-16.

When you're ready to start recording, click the Capture button and deal with the by now familiar Import Options dialog displayed in Figure 2-17. Specify where to save the clip, whether it should be a new Event or should be added to an existing Event (and which one), whether to split different days into different events, and whether to analyze for stabilization. Click the Capture button to proceed.

Figure 2-16:
Prepare
to capture
what the
iSight
can see.

Figure 2-17:
Set your
capture
options.

When you're finished, click Done to dismiss the Import From window and you'll see your new content in the Event Library.

We think that the Split Days into New Events check box is excess baggage here because live capture is almost never on different days, and if it is, it's still part of a single clip. The stabilization option is almost as redundant, but we suppose it's *possible* (although not likely) that you're carrying your MacBook while recording.

Importing video from other sources

As we mentioned earlier, we strongly recommend archiving your original content before erasing it from your camera. The File⇨Import⇨Camera Archive command lets you bring that footage into iMovie, either at a later date or, if you stored it on an external drive, on another Mac. Importing a camera archive is simple. Just follow these steps:

1. **Choose File⇨Import⇨Camera Archive.**

   A Save dialog, as shown in Figure 2-18, appears.

Figure 2-18:
iMovie
asks you
to locate
and select
a Camera
Archive.

2. **Navigate to and select the Camera Archive.**

3. **iMovie changes the instruction at the bottom of the dialog to tell you that you've selected the archive and should click Import to proceed, as shown in Figure 2-19.**

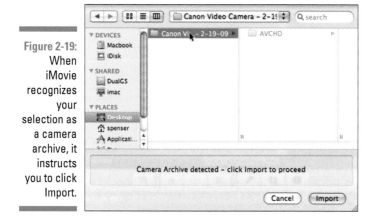

Figure 2-19: When iMovie recognizes your selection as a camera archive, it instructs you to click Import.

A progress dialog appears and then disappears when the import completes.

With a small archive, you'll miss the progress dialog if you blink – importing from a hard disk is fast.

4. **The Import From dialog now appears, just as if you had the named camera connected. Proceed as described earlier in this chapter for importing from a USB camera.**

You can also import content from compatible video files on your Mac's hard disk or external drives. Compatible files are MPEG-4, DV, and some QuickTime movie files (all but one of the ones we've tried worked, but Apple documents compatibility as "some .mov files"). Proceed as follows:

1. **Choose File⇨Import⇨Movies.**

A Save dialog appears, as shown in Figure 2-20.

2. **Tell iMovie where to save the clips, whether you're creating a new Event or augmenting an existing Event (and which one), how to deal with HD video, and whether the file should be copied (the original stays in place) or moved (the original is deleted after the file is copied).**

Figure 2-20:
Select your
movies
and set
your import
options
here.

3. **Click Import.**

   iMovie presents the Generating Thumbnails progress dialog shown in
   Figure 2-21. When done, you'll be back in the iMovie workspace with
   your new clips in the Event Library.

Figure 2-21:
iMovie
keeps you
informed of
its progress.

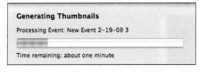

Similarly, you can import content from an existing iMovieHD project as
follows:

1. **Choose File➪Import➪iMovie HD Project.**

   A Save dialog appears, as shown in Figure 2-22.

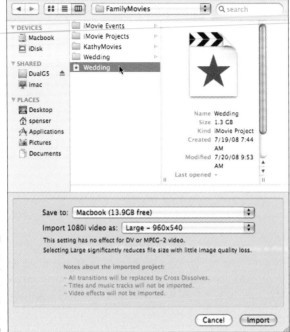

Figure 2-22:
Specify
the iMovie
project to
import.

2. **Select your iMovie HD project file and click Import.**

iMovie performs the conversion and keeps you informed of its progress.

Not everything comes over from an iMovie HD project when you import it. For example, all transitions come over as Cross Dissolve transitions (see Chapter 9 for more on Transitions). Titles and Effects (also covered in Chapter 9) are lost, and no music is transferred. Similarly, clips dragged into the iMovie HD project from the Finder do not come across either.

As we saw in Chapter 1, iMovie offers to bring compatible movies from iPhoto into your Event Library the first time you run iMovie. If you add other movies to your iPhoto Library or delayed the conversion, you can click the iPhoto Videos item in your Event Library and iMovie shows you compatible movies from which to choose.

3

Managing Events

*E*vents are the building blocks of iMovie. This chapter is all about how to manage Events: what they are, how to name them, organize them, and even how to archive them when you think you no longer need them.

Figuring Out What Events Are

In Chapter 2, we talk about the Event Library, iMovie's organizational structure that contains all your video clips. However, in that chapter, we don't get into exactly what an Event is, partly because an Event is whatever *you* want it to be. By default, as we show in a number of the screenshots in Chapter 2, iMovie suggests that footage shot on a single date be an Event (iPhoto has the same default for the images you import). Setting one day to equal one Event is, in our opinion, a pretty good default setting.

But if you want your weeklong Caribbean cruise to be an Event, you could designate the footage shot that entire week as a single Event. On the other hand, if you have a couple of kids in Little League who both have games on the same day, you probably want each game that you record to be a separate Event. iMovie's "each day is an Event" default works well enough for many situations, but you're free to override it whenever you want.

© iStockphoto/Steve Dangers

Naming Events

When you import video, iMovie suggests a default name for the Event — a combination of the words *New Event* and the date you imported the footage. We don't know about you, but the import date (possibly followed by a sequential number) is not how we think of Events. To us an Event is something like "Mom's 80th Birthday" or "Jessie's High School Graduation."

iMovie uses the import date, not the shoot date, as part of the suggested name. We don't really see why. If they were going to use a date as part of the name, why didn't they choose the shoot date? The date you shot the footage is obviously more meaningful to recognizing the Event than the day you finally got around to moving it from the camera to your Mac.

Although you can take iMovie's Event name suggestion, we feel that such a policy is only a slight improvement over leaving folder names as "Untitled-*n*," where *n* is the number that Finder adds by default. You should really pick a descriptive name for Events you're importing. We think the best time to do so is when you're importing the footage — after all, the content is right in front of you and fresh in your mind. Just replace the suggested text in the Import Options dialog (see Figure 3-1) and import your content.

Suggested name

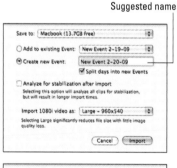

Figure 3-1:
iMovie
suggests a
name (top);
you supply a
meaningful
name
(bottom).

Supply your own name

If you neglect to change the name at import time, you can always go back and change the name later. Here's how:

1. **Show the Event Library if it is hidden.**

2. **Select the Event whose name you want to change, as shown in Figure 3-2.**

3. **Double-click the name to bring up a text box, as shown in Figure 3-3.**

4. **Type a new name and press Return or Enter.**

   Your Event is renamed, as shown in Figure 3-4.

Figure 3-2:
Select the
Event to
rename.

Figure 3-3:
Double-click
the name
to make it
editable.

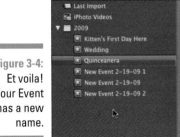

Figure 3-4:
Et voila!
Your Event
has a new
name.

Arranging Events

iMovie uses dates to organize the Event Library's Event list, and the items are organized by the year and, optionally, the month (View➪Group Events by Month) that the Event was added to the Event Library. Figure 3-5 shows the Event Library with grouping by month enabled. Notice that, even though a number of Events occurred in previous years (we added the year to the Event name to make the Events easier to locate), all the Events are listed as being in February, 2009, which is the month in which they were added to the Event Library. This presentation is a result of having View➪Most Recent Events at Top selected.

If you, like us, prefer to have your events chronological by occurrence, deselect View➪Most Recent Events at Top and the content is presented as shown in Figure 3-6.

You can give yourself more information about the Events by taking advantage of one of iMovie's Preference settings (iMovie➪Preferences or ⌘+,). Click the Browser icon at the top of the iMovie Preferences window to display the pane shown in Figure 3-7. Select the very first check box, Show Date Ranges in Event List, and your Event Library pane resembles that in Figure 3-8. (The Date Ranges in question are the first and last dates of the clips in the Event.)

Figure 3-5:
Your Event
Library is
sorted by
year and
month of
import.

Figure 3-6:
The Event
Library,
chrono-
logically
organized
by shooting
date.

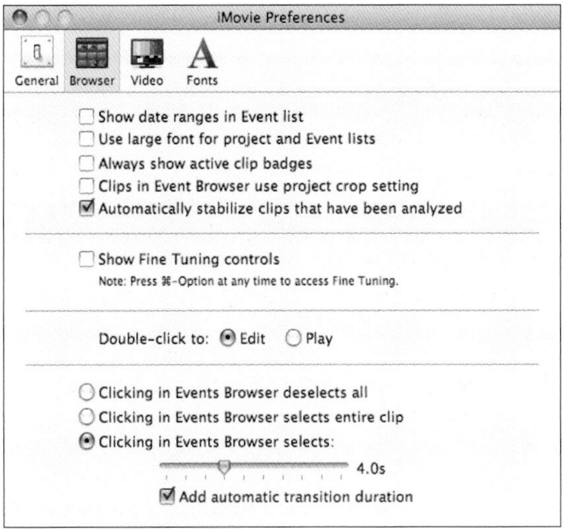

Figure 3-7:
The iMovie
Preferences'
Browser
pane.

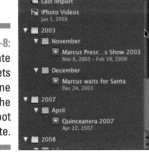

Figure 3-8:
Show Date
Ranges lets
you hone
in on the
actual shoot
date.

In our opinion, the chronological listing with date ranges displayed is the most efficient arrangement iMovie offers. Oddly enough, this arrangement comes close to mirroring the presentation in iPhoto. We wonder why the defaults are inconsistent between the two programs.

Moving, Copying, and Archiving Events

As you work with your iMovie footage and complete the projects that use it, you're probably going to want to free up some disk space rather than have old footage just laying around. Or, if you're like us and want to have back-up copies of your Events, you want to keep an extra copy (or more) on another disk for safety's sake. In either case, knowing how to move your Events around comes in very handy.

Figure 3-9 shows your Event Library displayed in the way to which you're already accustomed. That little iconic button in the right corner of the Event Library title bar is a disk icon. Click it to Group Events by Disk — the button turns blue when you're viewing Events by disk. The Event Library now displays all the disks your Mac knows about, as shown in Figure 3-10.

To copy an Event to another disk, proceed as follows:

1. **Click the disk button at the top-right of the Event Library to turn on Group by Disk.**

   The button turns blue and other disks your Mac knows about appear in the Event Library list.

2. **Select the Event or Events that you want to copy.**

3. **Drag them to the name of the disk where you want the copy to reside, as shown in Figure 3-11.**

   iMovie displays a progress dialog while it's making the copy. Copying large files from one disk to another can take a few minutes (or more), and video files tend to be large.

Disk icon

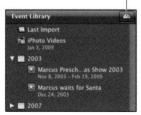

Figure 3-9: The normal Event Library display.

Figure 3-10: The Event Library with Group by Disk turned on.

Figure 3-11:
Drag the
Events to
the destina-
tion disk in
the Event
Library list.

Caution icon

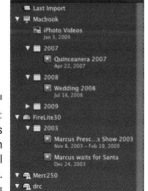

Figure 3-12:
Your Events
are now on
the external
disk.

When it's done, you have a duplicate of the Events on the second disk. If you want the files moved and the originals deleted (that is, if you're archiving the footage), hold down the ⌘ key in Step 3. Figure 3-12 shows the result of a move.

You may notice the little Caution triangle icons on two of my disks (Merc250 and drc at the bottom of the list) in the screenshots. These warn you that the disks are server volumes on another Mac and that the copy or move could be very time-consuming. Additionally, if the server volumes aren't mounted, you can't access the content.

4

Working with Clips

Say that you've shot your footage and imported it into your Event Library. Now it's time to get down to the nitty-gritty: Selecting the clips you want to use and editing them.

In this chapter, we delve into the techniques available for viewing your clips, marking clips as favorites (or rejects), designating which clips are displayed in the Event Library's clip pane, and employing iMovie's stabilization routines to eliminate the seismic shaking commonly seen in handheld camcorder video.

Finding Out About Clips

To get started, we have to define the word *clip* for the context of this (and any future) discussion: It's a word we've been using and about which we believe you probably have a general understanding. A *clip* is a continuous stream of video. In other words, from the time you start recording until you click the camera's Record button to stop it is one clip. If you subtract the time code for the beginning of a clip from the time code for the end of a clip, you get the length of your clip. Similarly, if you cut footage from the middle of a clip, the result is two shorter clips.

©iStockphoto/james steidl

DIRE

Time codes are a somewhat techy concept, but you find them discussed in many digital video contexts, so you probably ought to get a handle on the idea. Video is composed of *frames*, which are essentially still images. NTSC video has essentially 29.97 frames per second, but most people just count it as 30; PAL has 25 frames per second. If you think of video like a picture flipbook, with 30 pages per second flipping by, you'll understand why we see the video as a continuous stream. (In cartoon animation, for example, we know that if the rate of images moving by is more than about 16 frames per second, the human eye doesn't notice the discontinuities.) iMovie defaults to expressing time codes in the form *hh:mm:ss* (hours from 0–23, minutes from 0–59, and seconds from 0–59), but you can opt to show the frames (from 0–29 for NTSC or 0–24 for PAL) in the iMovie Preferences' General pane, shown in Figure 4-1 with the cursor pointing to the Display Time as HH:MM:SS:Frames check box.

Figure 4-2 shows the Event Library status bar when you don't have Frame display turned on at the top and with Frame display active on the bottom.

Because iMovie omits the hour field from the display when less than an hour is present, the 1:15:12 (which is for a clip that is 1 min, 15 sec, and 12 frames) displayed in Figure 4-2, out of context, could be misinterpreted to mean 1 hr, 15 min, and 12 seconds. We think that time codes should be fully exhibited because the frame display is optional. Because iMovie is targeted at endeavors shorter than an hour, Apple might argue that this implementation is unlikely to cause confusion, but how about those clips where the display shows, for example, 5:23? Is that 5 minutes, 23 seconds, or is it 5 seconds plus 23 frames? If frames were always displayed, we would know that the rightmost number was frames and no confusion could result from a shortened time code display.

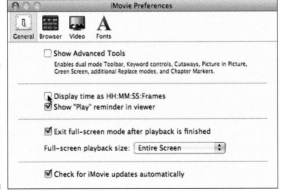

Figure 4-1:
Turn on
Frames
display in
iMovie's
General
Preferences.

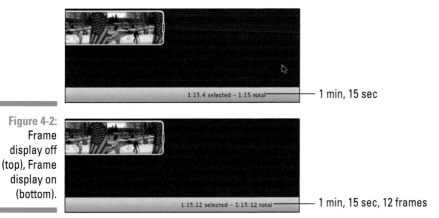

—— 1 min, 15 sec

—— 1 min, 15 sec, 12 frames

Figure 4-2:
Frame
display off
(top), Frame
display on
(bottom).

Viewing Clips in the Event Library

Some people don't edit their video in any way, shape, or form and they just put out the raw footage for others to see. Other than surveillance video, where you need to have a continuous stream, we don't see any reason to return to the boring, unedited, 8mm home movie days of the '40s (and a few other decades, since 8mm home video debuted in 1932). Why should you? iMovie makes it easy to eliminate unwanted material and fix problems like jitter. (Okay, laziness could be considered a reason by some, but we call it an excuse rather than a reason.)

To determine which clips and how much of those clips you want to use, you need to watch them. You also need to watch them to determine which require adjustments for color, cropping, audio problems, or jittery video. We cover stabilization (jittery video correction) later in this chapter, audio adjustments in Chapter 11, and other adjustments in Chapter 6.

You have essentially two ways to view your video in iMovie. The first is in the workspace and the second is full-screen, but both environments offer the same editing techniques.

When you select a clip in the Event Library, the clip gets a yellow border and sports a small Action badge (the gear and menu indicator) in the lower-left corner, with a time code above it, indicating the length of the selection. The Action badge displays a menu of actions (shown in Figure 4-3) you can perform on the clip.

We find it difficult to postpone satisfying our curiosity, so we're going to satisfy yours by showing you the results of choosing any of the four menu items. The gratification of finding out how to proceed from those points is going to have to wait a bit, however.

Choosing one of the first three items displays one of the Inspectors shown in Figure 4-4 (all three Inspector panes are shown). The Clip Inspector acquires additional powers when you're viewing a clip in the Project Library, which we discuss in Chapter 5.

Choosing Cropping & Rotation from the action menu adds some controls to the top of the Viewer, as seen in Figure 4-5.

Now that we've slaked your curiosity concerning the badge, we are going to introduce a pair of buzzwords you should know in order to carry on a conversation with others concerning clip viewing (which you'll probably do at, say, your next cocktail party):

- **Playhead:** The red vertical bar indicating the current position within a clip.

- **Scrubbing:** The action of sliding the mouse pointer over a clip, moving the playhead. Notice that the Viewer tracks the action. Apple often refers to the visual result of this action as *skimming*. You can see the playhead (sometimes called the *scrubber bar*) under the hand cursor in Figure 4-6.

Figure 4-3: Selected clips offer a choice of editing actions.

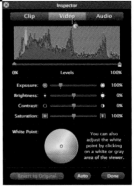

Figure 4-4: The Clip Inspector (top), the Audio Inspector (bottom left), and the Video Inspector (bottom right).

Figure 4-5: Cropping & Rotation controls in the Viewer pane.

Figure 4-6: iMovie displays the playhead's time code.

Viewing in the workspace

In the workspace, you scrub to position the playhead on the frame from which you want the clip to start playing. When you have the playhead positioned, press Space and the clip starts to play in the Viewer (press Space again to pause playback). You can also start and stop play by clicking the play button below the Event Library.

When you're scrubbing, a black cartoon dialog balloon appears indicating the playhead's time code, as shown in Figure 4-6. You might want to make note of some important time codes, such as where you want to trim your footage, split a clip, insert a clip, the spot you want to apply an effect, and so on.

Viewing full-screen

Switching to full-screen viewing in iMovie is, in our opinion, less straightforward than we've come to expect from iMovie (and Apple). There are four ways to enter full-screen mode. The method you select and when you select it affect what you see when you start viewing full-screen:

- You can click the Play Selected Events Full-Screen button below the Event Library. The clips in that Event start playing full-screen automatically from the beginning.

- You can choose Window⇨Show Events Full-Screen (⌘+7). The first frame of the first clip in the first selected Event appears full-screen, waiting for you to press Space to start it playing (or make the thumbstrip appear so that you can scrub to the point where you want play to begin). We say more on the thumbstrip in a couple of paragraphs.

✔ You can right-click (Control+click) the clip and choose Play Full-Screen from the contextual menu that appears. The clip starts playing full-screen from the where you right-clicked.

✔ You can choose View⇨Play full-screen (⌘+G) and, in most cases, the clip starts playing full-screen.

We say the clip starts playing full-screen "in most cases" because this menu item isn't really straightforward in indicating what is going to play. For example, if there is a project in the Project Library (we get into Projects in Chapter 5), the project is usually going to start playing, even if an Event is selected, but if the Event is already playing, pressing ⌘+G puts the Event playback into full-screen mode. If nothing has played yet and there is no project, iMovie just beeps at you. To add to this confusion, the tooltip that displays when you hover over the Play Selected Events Full-Screen button indicates that ⌘+G is the button's keyboard shortcut, and that doesn't mesh with the View⇨Play full-screen menu command. If this all seems a bit capricious to you, join the club. However, as long as you keep the oddities in mind as you work, you should be fine.

When viewing in full-screen mode, you can move the cursor toward the bottom of the screen to slightly reduce the viewing rectangle's size and display some additional controls (as we cover in Chapter 1). The most frequently employed control is what Apple calls the *thumbstrip:* that row of thumbnails immediately beneath the viewing rectangle. Just as in the Event Library's clip pane, you can scrub across the thumbstrip to position the video. Figure 4-7 shows the thumbstrip and the bottom of the viewing rectangle.

Figure 4-7:
Full-screen's thumbstrip lets you scrub to the desired frame.

iPhoto Videos - 19:24

The thumbstrip

Press Space to start playing (pressing Space while playing pauses playback). To exit full-screen mode, you can either move your cursor toward the bottom of the screen to display the controls and then click the circled X (shown here in the margin) in the bottom-left corner or, much more quickly, just press Esc.

Marking Favorites (and Rejects)

While viewing your video, you are quite likely to encounter footage that you really like, and also footage with which you're ashamed to be associated. iMovie makes it easy for you to mark both types of footage for later reference.

To mark video, proceed as follows:

1. **Select a range of frames, a clip, or multiple clips within an Event.**

2. **Press F to mark the video as a Favorite or R (or Delete) to indicate that it is a Reject (or press either the Mark Selection as Favorite button or the Reject Selection button, shown in the margin).**

   Footage that has been marked as a Favorite sports a green line at the top, as shown in Figure 4-8.

   Rejected footage, if your Show pop-up menu is set to All Clips or Rejected Only, displays a red line at the top, as shown in Figure 4-9; otherwise, it disappears from view.

A green line indicates a favorite.

Figure 4-8:
Look for the green line to find your favorite footage.

Red is for rejected.

Figure 4-9:
A red line signifies rejected video.

If you change your mind as to whether a video sequence is superb (or abysmal), select the range and press U or click the Unmark Selection button shown in the margin.

Hiding Clips

iMovie gives you four options as to which clips are shown when you select an Event. They are controlled by the Show pop-up menu beneath the Event Library as follows:

- **Favorites Only:** Just what the name implies — only footage marked as Favorites (described previously in this chapter) is visible. You should choose this option only after you have marked some Favorites; otherwise, you have no footage with which to work.

- **Favorites and Unmarked:** This is the default setting and displays all video that hasn't been rejected.

- **All Clips:** Displays all of your footage (rejected video sports a red bar at the top).

- **Rejected Only:** Displays only your rejects, sporting their signature red bar at the top.

The most common use of Favorites is to mark the footage you intend to use in your movie. After you've viewed all the video and marked what you want to use, it is a simple matter to choose Favorites Only from the Show pop-up menu and then drag the clips into your Project (see Chapter 5 for the lowdown on Projects).

Similarly, the most common use of Rejects is to mark the footage you want to dispose of. To dispose of the rejected video, choose File⇨Move Rejected Clips to Trash when you've completed viewing and marking your clips.

 Another way to utilize the Favorites and Rejects designators is to mark the footage you want in your movie as Favorites and the video for a blooper reel (or whatever you want to call your outtakes) as Rejects. With that accomplished, you can simply move the appropriate footage to the two different projects (we cover Projects in Chapter 5). More complex variations are possible using keywords, a feature of iMovie's Advanced Tools that we discuss in Chapter 6.

Stabilizing Clips

Sometimes, you want your video to be a bit jumpy, but those instances are certain to be intentional: conveying the sense of travelling over an uneven surface or simulating an earthquake are good examples of intentional shakiness. As a rule, though, you want a nice, steady frame of reference, where your subjects don't appear to have itching powder in their underwear. In Chapter 2, we recommended obviating the problem by using a tripod or Steadicam device. Lacking the availability of said equipment, iMovie features a stabilization adjustment that can (almost) make up for their absence. We qualify that with an "almost" because software can only work with the footage that's there. If your camera was shaking, you're prone to lose between "some" and "a lot" around the edges as the stabilized frames are constructed. With a camera that's stabilized in the first place, you get your full frame, every frame.

As we saw in Chapter 2, whenever you import material into iMovie, you're prompted about analyzing the video for stabilization. Figure 4-10 reprises the dialog you get before importing from a USB video camera, where you can see the check box asking whether to analyze.

After importing the video, iMovie presents a progress dialog while performing the analysis. Analyzing the video can be quite time-consuming — our informal tests showed slightly more than 5 minutes were required to analyze the 1 minute, 15 second clip from Figure 4-10. Other analyses we performed also yielded a 4:1 ratio of time spent analyzing versus length of clip on a 2.1GHz Core2Duo MacBook with 2GB of RAM. Thus, if you're going to import 45 minutes of video on a similarly configured system, plan on the analysis taking about 3 hours.

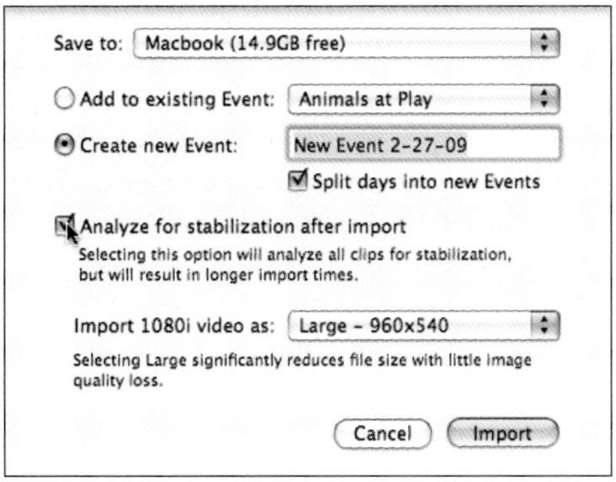

Figure 4-10:
If this check box is selected, you're asked whether to analyze for stabilization at every import.

Save to: Macbook (14.9GB free)

○ Add to existing Event: Animals at Play

◉ Create new Event: New Event 2-27-09

☑ Split days into new Events

☑ Analyze for stabilization after import
Selecting this option will analyze all clips for stabilization, but will result in longer import times.

Import 1080i video as: Large – 960x540

Selecting Large significantly reduces file size with little image quality loss.

Cancel   Import

And that length of time is for just the analysis. The actual stabilization isn't performed until you add the video to a project, as shown in the Inspector for our example clip, displayed in Figure 4-11. (Just to allay any concerns, the actual stabilization process when you add the clip to a project is hardly discernable.) We cover projects in Chapter 5.

Figure 4-11:
The actual stabilization takes place when the clip is added to a project.

Part II
Doing a Rough Cut

© iStockphoto/DNY59

In this part . . .

1n these four chapters, we cover the following topics:

✔ Chapter 5 gets you started working with iMovie's Project Library, creating projects, adding clips to a project, and organizing the clips in a project.

✔ Chapter 6 introduces iMovie's basic editing tools.

✔ Chapter 7 shows you how to work with still images in iMovie, including those photos you bring in from iPhoto and those that you create from frames in your video.

✔ Chapter 8 discusses iMovie's Themes, which are the supplied sets of transitions and titles that can give you a head start on presenting your movie.

Creating a Project

*W*hen we talk about *projects* in this book, we aren't using a polite euphemism for public housing. All your iMovie content exists in your Event Library, ready for use in your creative endeavors that we call movies. Hollywood doesn't call them *movies* or *motion pictures*, however, until they're released for public consumption (usually hyped beyond rational belief). Until the movie's release, however, the Industry calls them *projects*. When two directors meet, "What's your latest project?" is a question almost guaranteed to arise. Similarly, actors instruct their agents to find them a "good project."

We tend to think of a movie project in a manner similar to the way a Hollywood studio does: as the planning, scripting, casting, shooting, editing, and so forth that goes into producing our end result: a movie.

In this chapter, we explore what a project is, how to create a project, how to browse a project's content, and how to change default settings for a project. Additionally, we discuss how the Event Library lets you share clips between projects.

©iStockphoto/Andy Medina

What Is an iMovie Project?

When iMovie uses the word *Project*, the definition is much narrower than ours (or that of a movie studio). To iMovie, a project is where you assemble the video from your Event Library that you're going to transform into a movie.

The project is also where you add titles and transitions, apply special effects, tweak the audio, adjust the color, and make the edits that help your video tell the story you want told.

The adjustments made to your Project's video are local to that Project. This means that the adjustments you make while working on your Project don't appear in other Projects using that footage, nor are they reflected in the Event Library (the original footage's repository). This is called *non-destructive editing*: no matter how much you slice and dice and otherwise modify the video in a Project, the original footage remains intact.

Creating a Project

Your Project Library is seldom completely empty. The first time you launch iMovie, an unpopulated Project called *My First Project* resides in the Project Library, just waiting for your clips to move into the neighborhood, as shown in Figure 5-1. (Okay, so the housing project metaphor can be abused here.) If you delete all your completed projects and don't create a new one before you quit from iMovie, iMovie creates a My First Project placeholder the next time it runs. Therefore, the only way to have an empty Project Library is to delete all the projects, but the Project Library only stays empty until you quit.

If you ever wonder whether you're in the Project Library view or the Edit Project view, just check out the arrow: The view you're *not* in is the one named inside the arrow. Also, if the title bar just says Project Library, that's the view you're in. When you are editing a project, the Edit Project view's title bar includes the name of the project on which you're working; for example, *Project – My Coffee Break with Andre*.

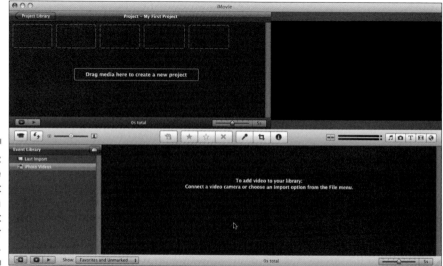

Figure 5-1:
iMovie
starts out
with a
Project
waiting for
your clips.

You can create a new Project in two ways:

- Choose File➪New Project (or press its keyboard equivalent, ⌘+N).
- Click the New Project button (the plus sign) at the bottom-right of the Project Library's pane.

In either case, iMovie displays the dialog shown in Figure 5-2, where you set some project properties, as follows:

- Give your project a name in the Project Name text box.
- Choose the aspect ratio from the aptly named Aspect Ratio pop-up menu. Your choices are Widescreen (16:9), Standard (4:3), and iPhone (3:2).

   Each aspect ratio is targeted at a specific common screen type. When the aspect ratios don't match, you see black bars either at each side of the video (pillarboxed), or at the top and bottom (letterboxed). Additionally, in the iMovie workspace, changing the aspect ratio resizes the Viewer pane, which in turn resizes the Project Library (or Event Library) pane to the Viewer's left.

- Choose a theme to set default styles and transitions for your movie, based upon professionally designed themes provided by Apple. We discuss themes in much greater detail in Chapter 8. The default theme setting for a new project is no theme at all.

- Specify whether you want iMovie to automatically add a transition between your clips by selecting the Automatically Add check box and then choosing your favorite transition from the adjoining pop-up menu.

- Click Create when you have everything the way you want it.

Figure 5-2: Establish initial Project settings in the New Project dialog.

Project Name: New Project
Aspect Ratio: Widescreen (16:9)
Theme:
None   Photo Album   Bulletin Board
Comic Book   Scrapbook   Filmstrip
Automatically add: Cross Dissolve
Cancel   Create

The subtle arrow outline in the Project Library's title bar (in the upper left of Figure 5-1) may have escaped your notice. Clicking in it moves you back and forth between the Edit Project view, where you work on the current project, and Project Library view, where you select the project on which you want to work.

Now that you've created a project, you're ready to move your favorite footage into said project. Select the clip or clips you want in the Event Library and drag them into the Project Library. A green vertical bar appears in the Project Library where the first selected clip comes to rest. An orange horizontal bar appears at the bottom of frames in the Event Library when they're being used in a project, as shown in Figure 5-3.

A red squiggle appears near the bottom of any footage that was too shaky for iMovie to stabilize, as shown in Figure 5-4. Once again, we urge you to use a tripod or other stabilizing hardware when shooting whenever possible. Otherwise, it's really easy to record video that is too erratic for iMovie's stabilization routines. If you look back at Figure 5-3, you can see a new button at the bottom of the Event Library to hide or show clip segments that are too shaky to stabilize: The red squiggle indicates that they're shown, a gray squiggle means they're hidden. If you don't want the shaky video to be moved to the project, hide the shaky video before dragging your video. Hiding the shaky video effectively splits the clip at the boundaries of the shaky sections, turning one clip into two, or three, or more clips, depending on the number of shaky sections that are hidden.

Be aware that hiding the shaky video can produce some discontinuity in your footage. You have to decide whether having some shaky video is worth it to include all the action and dialogue in your movie.

Note also that hiding shaky video in an Event clip after you add it to a Project does not affect the video in the Project. If the video had shaky sections when you added it to the Project, the shaky sections remain even after you hide them in the Event library.

Figure 5-3:
The Event
Library
marks
footage
used in
projects with
an orange
stripe at the
bottom.

Figure 5-4:
Red squig-
gles appear
in three
frames
indicating
video too
shaky to
stabilize.

Figure 5-4:
Red squig-
gles appear
in three
frames
indicating
video too
shaky to
stabilize.

Although dragging your clips into the Project is the simplest and most straightforward method of adding clips to your project for most occasions, iMovie provides another option via its Add to Project button. Proceed as follows:

1. **Select the frames you want to add to your project.**

2. **Click the Add Selection to Project button (shown in the margin) or press E.**

    iMovie adds the selection to the end of your project.

Because the selection is added at the end of the project, you may need to then move it to its proper position in the video sequence.

If you are going to move many different sequences into your project, you might want to turn on Advanced Tools in iMovie Preferences' General pane, as shown in Figure 5-5. Then, when you click the Add to Project button, it stays selected and you can make selection after selection, each of which is added to the end of the project, without having to click the button or press E each time.

Figure 5-5:
Turning on
Advanced
Tools in
iMovie
Preferences.

Changing a Project's defaults

You can rename the Project by double-clicking its name in the Project Library and typing a new name. You can also revisit the other settings at any time by choosing File⇨Project Properties (⌘+J), or by right-clicking in the Project Library and choosing Project Properties from the contextual menu that appears. (You can also right-click in a Project Browser pane to display the Project Properties dialog.) The Project Properties dialog drops down out of the title bar, as shown in Figure 5-6. The General pane is virtually identical to the New Project dialog, as you can see by comparing Figures 5-2 and 5-6.

Figure 5-6:
The Project
Properties
General
pane lets
you change
your mind
about what
you set
in New
Project.

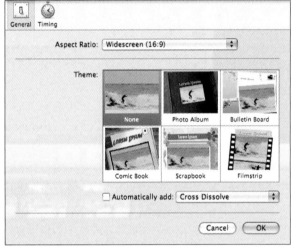

When iMovie creates a *My First Project*, you don't see the New Project dialog, and all the settings are defaults: The name is *My First Project*, the aspect ratio is Widescreen, the Theme is None, and automatic transitions are not in effect. If that's not what you want, you don't have to create a new project: Just press ⌘+J to display the Project Properties dialog and make any desired changes.

Browsing the Project

While working on your project, you're going to find yourself going back and forth through your video, checking for material you want to edit, places where you want to add audio or titles, or points where you want to insert additional content. Last, but far from least, you'll want to play your video to check out how well you're doing in molding your movie.

iMovie offers numerous ways to play your video, most of which are most easily accomplished with one finger on the keyboard, as described in the following list:

- ✔ **View➪Play.** The keyboard shortcut is to press Space. Pressing Space starts your video playing from the playhead location. If you haven't positioned the playhead, your project starts playing from the beginning.

- ✔ **View➪Play Selection.** The keyboard shortcut is to press / (slash). If you haven't made a selection, play commences from the project's beginning.

- ✔ **View➪Play from Beginning.** The keyboard shortcut is to press \ (backslash).

- ✔ **View➪Play Around Current Frame➪1 Second** and **View➪Play Around Current Frame➪3 Seconds.** The keyboard shortcuts are [and] (left and right square bracket), respectively. The current frame is a somewhat nebulous concept. When you have selected something, the current frame is the first frame of the selection. Lacking a selection, the current frame is the first frame of the segment of the specified length centered around the playhead.

- ✔ **Click the Play button at the bottom of the Project Library pane**. This is equivalent to pressing Space.

You can freeze the playhead's position by pressing Control before moving the cursor to the menu bar or Play button, but pressing the keyboard shortcut is much more efficient.

 We recommend using the Swap Events and Projects button (see the margin) to place the Projects pane in the iMovie workspace's more spacious bottom pane when you're working on a project, and switching them back to the defaults when you're working in the Event Library.

Sharing Events between Projects

The most memorable real-life events may be once-in-a-lifetime occurrences, but the best iMovie Events are the ones you can reuse across multiple Projects.

As we noted earlier in this chapter, Event footage that has been added to a Project sports an orange line along the bottom in the Event Library's clips pane. As long as the frames in question are used in at least one project on your Mac, that line remains. When the line disappears, you know that it's safe to archive and delete the footage, if you wish, or make permanent changes.

Changes made to video in a project exist only in that project. An Event's video can appear in multiple projects with different adjustments, titles, and so on. This is why, for example, that you analyze Event video for stabilization, but iMovie doesn't actually stabilize the footage until it's in a project: The same Event video in different projects can have different stabilization settings. We cover basic editing in Chapter 6 and transitions and advanced editing in Part III.

6

Video Editing Basics

Say you have all kinds of raw material at your disposal, just waiting to be used in your magnum opus. But as you peruse your source material, you realize that using everything makes your movie too long and that some of the footage has dull colors, poor audio, or is just plain not of the quality you demand. Finally, you decide that you need to add narration or background audio to some frames to introduce what's going on or set a mood.

iMovie lets you perform the modifications necessary to resolve the above issues, up to a point. iMovie lets you trim, polish, and adorn your video, but even iMovie isn't an alchemist: You can't use it to turn lead into gold and it won't help you turn bad footage into an Oscar-worthy movie or documentary. Remember, even Hitchcock and Spielberg have produced some clunkers when the acting or script weren't up to par, but those movies would have been far worse without their expert touch.

© iStockphoto/Shannon Matteson

In this chapter, we introduce you to iMovie's Advanced Tools, the use of keywords to identify and classify clips, trimming and editing clips in your project, and adjusting the color and audio in your project.

Introducing iMovie's Advanced Tools

Apple calls these tools "Advanced," but we think that they relieve the drudgery and simplify assembling our movies. To turn on Advanced Tools, proceed as follows:

1. **Choose iMovie⇨Preferences, or press the keyboard equivalent, ⌘+, (comma).**

2. **If the General pane is not selected, click the General icon in the toolbar.**

3. **Select the Show Advanced Tools check box, as shown in Figure 6-1.**

4. **Click the iMovie Preferences window's close button (or press ⌘+W).**

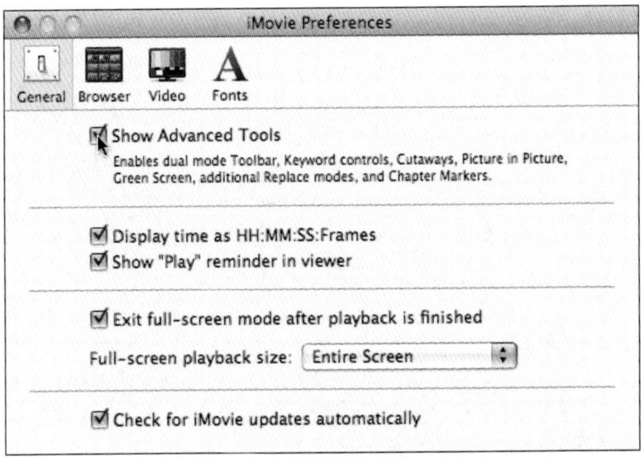

Figure 6-1:
Turn on
Advanced
Tools in the
General
Preferences
pane.

Your toolbar sprouts a couple of new buttons, an Arrow button and a Keywords button, as well as a Show or Hide Keyword Filtering pane button beneath the Event Library. You can see these buttons in Figure 6-2. Advanced Tools also modifies the operation of the Add to Project button, the Mark as Favorite button, the Unmark button, and the Reject button.

Normally (that is, when you haven't turned on Advanced Tools), you make a selection and then click the button for the action you wish to perform. When Advanced Tools are active, you click the button for the desired tool and then make selections until you're done with the tool, at which point you click the Arrow button to turn the tool off. Deselecting the tools is the only function the Arrow button performs: Think of it as an "off" switch.

If you make a selection in the Event Library before selecting a tool while using Advanced Tools, you see the Add to Project, Mark as Favorite, Unmark, and Reject buttons sprout plus (+) signs in their upper-right corners, as shown in Figure 6-3. When the + signs are present, Advanced Tool mode is suspended, and the toolbar buttons revert to their normal behavior. Apple refers to this behavior as the *dual mode toolbar*. To resume Advanced Tools operation, click anywhere in the gray areas of the Event Library or Project Library, which deselects anything that was selected, and the plus signs disappear.

Why does iMovie use a plus sign to indicate that Advanced Tools is suspended? It seems, at least to us, that a minus sign would be more appropriate. The first time Dennis saw the Advanced Tools, he happened to have an active selection, so he thought the plus sign indicated some additional (that is, more advanced) capability, until he found the explanation in iMovie Help. Nope: It's just an iMovie quirk for which we really don't know the explanation.

Arrow button   Keywords button

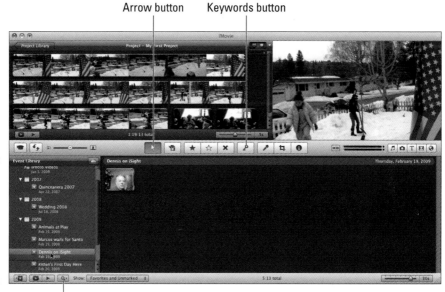

Figure 6-2: Advanced Tools adds three buttons to the iMovie workspace.

Show/Hide Keyword Filtering Pane button

Figure 6-3: Advanced Tools operation is temporarily suspended.

Plus signs mean advanced mode is suspended.

Discovering the Keywords dialog

Apple evidently intended iMovie's keywords functionality to be analogous to the one in iPhoto as a way to indicate categories for your footage. The pre-supplied keywords are Indoor, Outdoor, Landscape, Closeup, Wide Angle, People, and Pets. Click the Keywords button in the toolbar to display the Keywords dialog shown in Figure 6-4. Click the tab for the pane you want near the top of the Inspector.

Footage with one or more associated keywords sports a light blue (or dare we say, *aqua*) bar near the top.

Add your own keywords to the list by typing the new keyword in the New Keyword text box at the bottom of the Keywords Auto-Apply pane, or by making a selection and then typing the new keyword in the Keyword text box at the bottom left of the Keywords Inspector.

You can reorder the list in the Keywords dialog by selecting a keyword and dragging it to the new position — a blue line tracks your drag, showing you where the repositioned keyword will be. Because the numeric keyboard shortcuts (listed at the right of the rows) apply to only the first 9 items in the list, placing your most frequently used keywords at or near the top of the list makes them more accessible. Reordering performed in either pane is reflected in the other. Notice that the keyboard shortcuts are still sequential, so if you drag Pets to the second position on the list, its shortcut changes from 7 to 2. The shortcuts for Outdoor through People change in increments of 1.

If you intend to tag a number of frame sequences with the same keywords, select those keywords in the Auto-Apply pane and then start selecting your footage. All selected keywords are automatically associated with the video.

Figure 6-4:
The
Keywords
dialog. The
Auto-Apply
pane is
on the left
and the
Inspector
pane is on
the right.

Alternatively, if you wish to apply keywords on an ad hoc basis as you skim through your video, proceed as follows:

1. **Select your footage.**

2. **Open the Keywords Inspector by clicking the Keywords toolbar button.**

3. **Select the check boxes for keywords you want applied.**

   iMovie shows a minus sign in the check boxes of any keywords currently applied to part, but not all, of the footage, and a check mark in the boxes where the keyword applies to the whole selection.

4. **Click Add to Clip.**

   Pressing Option while clicking a keyword in the Auto-Apply Inspector applies the keyword to the entire clip, which saves you from having to drag-select the entire clip.

If you want to remove all keywords from selected frames, press 0 (zero). This method is a lot faster than showing the Keywords Inspector, selecting all the check boxes, and clicking the Remove All button.

Filtering by keyword

Although you can certainly follow Apple's lead in how to use keywords, we'd be remiss if we didn't give you some food for thought about additional ways to exploit the keyword functionality. In Chapter 3, we mention that you can use keywords to identify blooper-reel material so that, when it comes time to create your blooper reel project, you can easily find all the blooper reel footage and click Add to Project. Assuming that you have already associated the Blooper keyword with your designated frames, here's how to proceed:

1. **Click the Show Filter by Keywords button to display the Filter by Keyword pane, as shown in Figure 6-5.**

Figure 6-5:
Show the Filter by Keyword pane to find your tagged footage.

2. **Select the keyword or keywords for which you want to find the tagged frames and select the green (right) side of the button next to the keyword's name in the Filter by Keyword pane.**

   You can exclude video tagged with a keyword from the footage searched by clicking the red (left) side of the lozenge-shaped button to the left of the keyword. You might do this, for example, when you want to find scenes tagged as Outdoor that aren't candidates for the blooper reel: Exclude the Blooper keyword and then filter for Outdoor scenes. You might also want to exclude all blooper reel material from the selected footage so that you can add the remainder to your project.

3. **Click the Any button at the bottom of the Filter by Keyword pane if you want to find all frames tagged with any of the selected keywords (an "or" search). Click the All button if you wish to find the frames that have every selected keyword applied (an "and" search).**

   The clips pane to the right displays the footage your filter identifies.

At the time we're writing this, there is an anomaly (that's polite talk for "bug") in the Filter by Keyword pane's operation. The first keyword to appear in the list allows only the red side (the "not" side) to be selected, so you can only exclude footage with that keyword. Our temporary workaround is to create a dummy keyword, which we call "00placeholder" because iMovie presents the Filter by Keywords pane's entries in alphanumeric order. Then, we just don't tag any footage with it, nor do we include it in any of our filters. Hopefully, Apple fixes this problem by the time you read this material, but if not, you now have a workaround.

Previewing Your Clips

We covered viewing your clips in Chapter 4, but that was to discover the available techniques and to get a general sense of what you have in your Events. Here, you've selected the footage you want and included it in your project. Now, you're going to start transforming this collection of clips into the story you want to tell.

Sourcing material from different Events

One common example of pulling footage from different Events is for the venerable "highlight reel." Whether you're compiling "Best of" moments for your holiday video to friends and family (the 21st century version of the traditional Christmas letter) or a "funniest moments" short taken from your kids' antics and activities over the years, you will find yourself extracting clips from different Events.

You might have an urge to combine Events to more closely parallel your projects. Please restrain yourself if there is *any* possibility that you might want to use footage from one of the Events in more than one project, such as the main project for which it was intended as well as a highlights video or some other compilation.

iMovie makes it very easy to select your clips from multiple Events, especially if you make use of keywords as described earlier in this chapter. Tag your footage, select all the Events in question, and then use Filter by Keyword to collect the video from multiple Events to add to your project with one click of the Add to Project button (or one press of the E key).

Arranging your footage

When new clips are added to a project, they're added to the end. While you're skimming through your video, keep an eye out for where the new clips actually belong. Move the clips into position and then preview again to see what else, if anything, needs to be done. For example, you might decide you need a title to introduce the scene or a transition into the clip (see Chapter 9 for coverage of titles and transitions). Or, you might decide that you want to trim a few frames off one end or the other: We almost always have a few seconds of extra footage at either end of our clips, as discussed in Chapter 2, to make sure that we don't start filming too late or stop too soon. It is always easy to trim what isn't needed, but well-nigh impossible to fill in for something that just doesn't exist!

You can drag footage from the Event Library and position it precisely within existing footage. When you drag the footage to the desired position and release the mouse button, you see the preceding menu. Choose the option you wish by clicking it. The Cutaway, Picture in Picture, and Green Screen choices might not be immediately obvious, but we discuss them in more detail in Chapter 10.

Adjusting Your Video

iMovie's non-destructive editing really makes your job easier when it comes to trimming clips, performing color adjustments, and so forth. iMovie offers a number of adjustment possibilities: They are performed, as is the case with most of Apple's software, in the Inspector. You can invoke the Inspector in a number of ways. The most common ways to do so are

- ✔ Double-click in a clip. The Inspector appears, as shown in Figure 6-6. If you are working with video that has a different aspect ratio than the project, the Clip Inspector tells you that you have to convert the clip before you can apply a speed adjustment.

- ✔ Click the Inspector button in the toolbar (seen here in the margin).

- ✔ Choose Window➪Clip Adjustments, Window➪Video Adjustments, or Window➪Audio Adjustments, or their respective keyboard shortcuts: I, V, or A.

Personally, we're partial to the keyboard shortcuts and double-clicking as the fastest and easiest methods of accessing the Inspector. The keyboard shortcuts are especially efficient because they take you directly to the Inspector pane you want. You can also use the keyboard shortcuts to switch between Inspector panes while the Inspector is open.

Figure 6-6:
The Inspector's
Clip pane
before con-
verting the
clip (left),
and after
(right).

Exploring clip adjustments

When working with project clips, the Clip Inspector has four sections: Duration, Video Effect, Speed, and Stabilization.

Working with project clips differs from working with Event clips. Changes made to clips in the Event Browser carry over into any project that uses those clips, but editing performed in a project is local to that project.

The Duration section is intended primarily for setting the duration of still images (such as photos) added to your project, and we talk about that in more detail in Chapter 7. For video, typing a new duration shortens the clip to the specified length by truncating — if you type a duration longer than the source clip's length, iMovie sets the duration back to the source clip's duration.

Clicking the Video Effect button rotates the Inspector to display the Choose Video Effect dialog shown in Figure 6-7. The thumbnails represent the effect applied to your clip; you can also preview the effect in the Viewer as you skim across the thumbnail. Return to the Clip Inspector by clicking the effect you want or by clicking Cancel (pressing Esc is the same as clicking Cancel).

The effect you choose is visible in the Viewer when previewing your footage, but the only indication that an effect has been applied to a clip is a small circled i Inspector badge in the upper-left corner of the clip's initial thumbnail, as shown in Figure 6-8. And, to make the visual effect's presence even less obvious, the badge is only visible when the clip is selected and the playhead is in the clip. We cover Video Effects in much more detail in Chapter 9.

The Speed section is where you speed up or slow down your video (fast action and slo-mo) or reverse a clip's direction so that it plays backward. You can combine reverse direction with either fast- or slo-mo. Use the slider or the text boxes visible in Figure 6-6 (on the right) to adjust the clip's speed either by a percentage (top text box) or to make it fit in a specified duration (bottom text box). Not to belabor the obvious, select the Reverse check box to make your clip play backward.

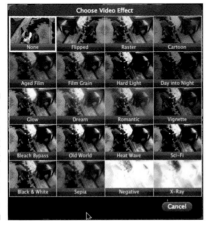

Figure 6-7:
Select a
visual effect
you want
applied to
your clip
here.

Figure 6-8:
A clip with a
dark back-
ground can
make you
miss the
visual effect
indicator in
the upper-
left corner.

Indicates an effect has been applied.

The Stabilization section lets you specify that iMovie should attempt to smooth the motion in shaky video. Additionally, if the clip hasn't yet been analyzed for stabilization, selecting the Smooth clip motion check box initiates the analysis.

Adjusting your video's color

Open the Video Inspector by pressing V, choosing Window⇨Video Adjustments, or (if the Inspector is open) by clicking the Inspector's Video tab. When it's open, you see the large and colorful Inspector shown in Figure 6-9.

Histogram Highlights slider

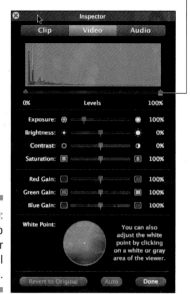

Figure 6-9:
The Video
Inspector
is a colorful
toolshop.

For those of you familiar with iPhoto's adjustment tools (or Photoshop's), using the Video Inspector should be a very comfortable exercise. The histogram (the graph at the top), displays the levels of red, green, and blue in your frame's shadows (left), midtones (center), and highlights (right).

For those of you as yet unfamiliar with the tools presented here, we offer this brief rundown:

- **The Histogram Highlights slider:** This slider is the one on the right with the white bar below the triangle. Use it to narrow the range between shadows and highlights, thus spreading the colors out more. Moving the shadow slider to the right darkens the image; moving the highlights slider to the left lightens the image. This is called a *Levels adjustment*.

  Alternatively, you can let iMovie take its best shot at making the adjustment by clicking the Auto button at the bottom of the Video Inspector.

- **Exposure:** Drag this slider to the left to darken the shadows or to the right to intensify the highlights.

- **Brightness:** Dragging Brightness to the left darkens the image and dragging it to the right brightens the image.

- **Contrast:** Dragging Contrast to the right increases the range between the darkest and lightest colors (intensifying the edges between light and dark areas), whereas dragging to the left reduces the range of colors between the darkest and lightest (making the edges less distinct).

- **Saturation:** Dragging Saturation to the left drains the color from an image, reducing it to a grayscale rendition, whereas dragging to the right intensifies the image's colors.

- **Red, Green, and Blue Gain:** Visible only when you have Advanced Tools enabled, these sliders let you dull (left) or intensify (right) each component color individually.

- **White Point:** Clicking in the color wheel tells iMovie to make the clicked color a new white point, thus changing all the colors accordingly. You can also set a new white point by clicking on an appropriate white (or gray) area in the Viewer, which is our recommended method. Changing the white point is especially useful in removing color casts that arise when the camera is not adjusted for the type of lighting in use (for example, incandescent lighting tends toward an orange cast and natural sunlight tends toward a blue cast).

Again, thanks to iMovie's non-destructive editing, if you don't like the results of your changes, you can always revert the video to its original color state, simply by clicking Revert to Original at the bottom-left of the Video Inspector.

Making audio adjustments

No matter how much we (or you) discuss iMovie as a video tool, you need to remember that without audio, we'd be back in the days of silent pictures. (Actually, we'd be back in the zoetrope or nickelodeon era: As soon as motion pictures got into theaters, the theater owners had pianists playing mood music to fit the current scenes.) Dialogue, sound effects, and background music are critical aspects of a successful modern movie.

Display the Audio Inspector by choosing Window⇨Audio Adjustments, pressing A, or (if the Inspector is already open) by clicking the Audio tab. The Audio Inspector is shown in Figure 6-10.

Figure 6-10:
Adjust your
selection's
audio here.

The Audio Inspector offers the following adjustments:

- ✔ **Volume:** The volume adjustment is intuitively obvious. You drag the slider to the left to reduce the volume (0 percent is Mute) or to the right to increase the volume, up to a maximum of 200 percent.

- ✔ **Ducking:** iMovie lets you have multiple audio tracks — for example, sound effects, background music, or narration — playing simultaneously with your video's actual audio. This is accomplished by lowering the volume of other tracks, also known as *ducking.* Click the Reduce Volume of Other Tracks check box to turn ducking on. By default, other tracks have their volume reduced to 15 percent of normal. You can adjust the amount of ducking with the slider.

The term *ducking* is a piece of jargon from the pop music business. We find it a little odd that Apple chose to use this term, but has so strenuously endeavored to remove other bits of industry jargon from iMovie. For example, they say *skimming* instead of *scrubbing, pointer* instead of *playhead* (which is especially confusing given all of the other uses for pointer), and so forth.

✓ **Fade In/Fade Out:** By default, audio ramps up from 0 to full volume in the first half-second of a clip (15 frames for NTSC or ATSC) and down from 100 percent to Mute in the last half-second. Selecting the Automatic radio button employs the default. To take control, either click the Manual radio button and adjust the slider from 0 frames to 2 seconds, or just drag the slider, which automatically selects the Manual radio button (pun intended).

✓ **Normalize Clip Volume:** This adjustment is specifically meant for situations where you have multiple clips selected and the volume varies significantly between them. Click Normalize Clip Volume and iMovie adjusts the respective sound levels until they are approximately equal. You can select clips and click Remove Normalization to revert a clip's volume.

 Clips with audio adjustments applied sport a small speaker badge in their upper-left corner when they are selected, as shown in the margin. You can double-click the badge to go immediately to the Audio Inspector.

7

Working with Stills

*S*peaking of stills, we'll take a jug of that White Lightning, please . . . whoops, wrong kind of still. From the early zoetropes and kinetoscopes through to today's IMAX and Blu-Ray, video really boils down to a series of still images passing so quickly through our vision that our minds perceive continuous motion.

Still images, however, still have value in movies beyond their fleeting passage as a frame of video. Numerous movies (for example, *Hello, Dolly!*) and TV shows (such as *NCIS*) have employed frozen images to lead into a scene or close out a scene, or both. Ken Burns's documentaries on PBS, where still images of historic events are brought to life through panning and zooming, did a lot to popularize the documentary far beyond PBS's normal audience. Using iMovie's Ken Burns Effect, you can achieve the same effects in your movies.

©iStockphoto/Lee Pettet

Another common use of still images in video is the "news commentary," where a photograph fills the screen while audio commentary continues. Yet another is the venerable slideshow, a staple in so many pieces of software (iPhoto, iDVD, Photoshop, Keynote, and others ad nauseum).

As you make more movies, or even as you watch more movies and television with an eye toward how they are put together, you will find all sorts of situations where a still image is just what the producer prescribed. In this chapter, we fill you in on iMovie's still image toolbox.

Extracting a Frame for Use As a Still

As we mentioned in the introduction to this chapter, a frozen frame to introduce or conclude a scene is an often-used and very effective technique. Extracted still frames are called *freeze frames* because they present a moment frozen in time. To freeze a frame of your video project, proceed as follows:

1. **Position the playhead at the frame you want to extract.**

2. **Hold down the Control key and click to display the contextual menu shown in Figure 7-1.**

3. **Choose Add Freeze Frame from the menu.**

   iMovie creates a four-second still clip at the playhead's position.

You could also right-click to present the contextual menu in Step 2, but you then risk accidentally clicking on a frame other than the one you want to freeze. Pressing Control locks the playhead while you move your mouse pointer. (This is the first time Dennis recalls encountering a situation where Control-clicking is clearly preferable to right-clicking.) The fact that you need to press Control to lock the playhead's position anyway is probably the rationale for having Freeze Frame available only via a contextual menu.

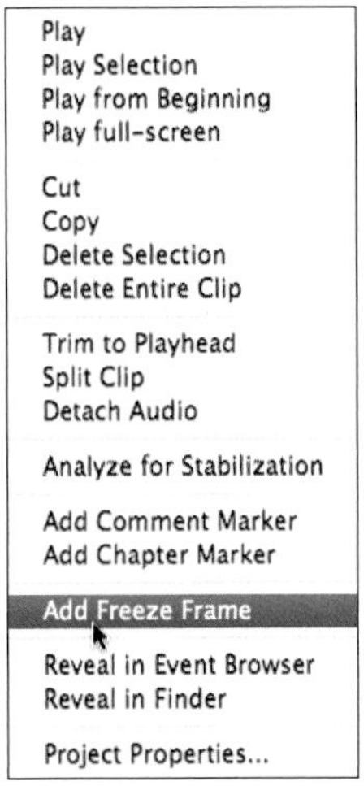

Figure 7-1:
Choose
Freeze
Frame to
create your
still clip.

Play
Play Selection
Play from Beginning
Play full-screen

Cut
Copy
Delete Selection
Delete Entire Clip

Trim to Playhead
Split Clip
Detach Audio

Analyze for Stabilization

Add Comment Marker
Add Chapter Marker

Add Freeze Frame

Reveal in Event Browser
Reveal in Finder

Project Properties...

If you want to add a freeze frame from your Event Library to your project, the following steps walk you through the (rather short) process:

1. **Position the playhead at the frame you want in the Event Browser.**

2. **Hold down the Control key and click to display the contextual menu shown in Figure 7-2.**

Figure 7-2:
Choose Add
Still Frame
to Project
to bring a
frame from
your Event
Library into
the project.

Play
Play Clip
Play from Beginning
Play full-screen

Select Entire Clip

Adjust Clip Date and Time...

Split Event Before Clip
Add Still Frame to Project

Reveal in Finder

Project Properties...

3. **Choose Add Still Frame to Project from the menu.**

    iMovie adds a four-second still frame clip to the end of your project. Feel free to position it where you want it, as described in Chapter 6.

When you add a still frame clip to your project using the preceding steps, iMovie automatically applies the Ken Burns Effect to the clip. To convert the clip to a true freeze frame, you need to remove the Ken Burns Effect. We explain more about this effect later in this chapter in the section, "Applying the Ken Burns Effect."

If you want a freeze frame duration other than four seconds, you can change the still clip's length in the Clip Inspector, as we describe later in this chapter in the section, "Adjusting Duration."

One technique frequently employed with freeze frames is to apply a video effect, such as Black & White or Sepia, in the Clip Inspector and to either play a short riff as audio accompaniment to set the mood or to start playing the background music during the freeze frame and continuing it into the actual video. Experiment with variations of this technique to see what best suits your artistic vision. We cover iMovie's Video Effects in Chapter 9, in case you want to jump ahead.

Adding a Still Image to Your Project

iLife's integration provides a service available to other applications on your Mac — the Media Browser. Through the Media Browser, you can access the content in your iTunes and iPhoto Libraries, as well as GarageBand and iMovie projects in whatever program you're running (so long as its developers included Media Browser support, for example, Apple's iWork suite of applications, Roxio Toast Titanium, and Disc Cover).

 Click the Photos button (shown in the margin) in the iMovie workspace's toolbar, and iMovie opens the Media Browser pane in the lower-right corner of the workspace, as shown in Figure 7-3.

If the disclosure triangle to the left of the iPhoto item is pointing to the right, click it (the triangle now points down) and your iPhoto Library's Events, Photos, and albums — both regular and smart albums — appear in the pane. If you select Events, you can skim the cursor over the thumbnails at the bottom of the Photos pane to get a preview of the photos in that Event. Double-click the Event to show thumbnails of all its photos in the bottom portion of the Photos pane (drag up or down on the dividing bar to reapportion the space between the list and the thumbnail areas). Use the Search box at the bottom to locate photos based on name, keyword, or any other text-based criterion (for example, Description) that you've entered in iPhoto. You can also use the check box and associated pop-up menu in the status bar below the Photos pane to restrict the display to photos whose dates fall within a specified date range around a selected Event. (Your choices are same date(s), within one day, within one week, and within one month.) The magnification slider to the pop-up's right gives you control over the size of the thumbnails.

Click to see iPhoto Library contents if they're not already visible.

Figure 7-3: The Media Browser's Photo pane gives you access to your iPhoto Library.

Select the photo (or photos) you want and drag their thumbnails to your project.

Cropping (and Rotating) Stills

If you use still images in your projects, and we wager that most of you do so with varying degrees of frequency, you're going to encounter situations where you only want to use part of the photo. Or maybe the photo you want to use has a portrait orientation when you want landscape to match the movie's aspect ratio. You could go back to iPhoto (if that was the source of your image) and make changes, but iMovie also offers you cropping and rotation capabilities, and it is all non-destructive, which means that you can continue to tweak the image within iMovie and not have to keep going back and forth between applications. The cropping and rotation tools are available in the Viewer, along with the Ken Burns Effect, which we cover later in this chapter.

As usual, iMovie offers you more than one way to make the crop, rotation, and Ken Burns Effect tools appear in the Viewer. These methods are

 ✔ Click the Crop, Rotate, and Ken Burns tool button in the iMovie toolbar. You can see the button in the margin.

 ✔ Choose Window⇨Cropping, Ken Burns & Rotation.

 ✔ Double-click the crop badge at the upper left of the clip's thumbnail in your project.

 ✔ Press the keyboard shortcut, C.

 ✔ Click a clip's Action menu (the gear-like badge that appears when you hover your mouse pointer near the beginning of the clip) and choose Cropping, Ken Burns, & Rotation from the menu that appears.

Seven buttons now overlay the top of the Viewer pane, as shown in Figure 7-4. From left to right, these buttons are:

 ✔ **Fit:** Click this button to have iMovie display the entire image within the frame. This usually results in letterboxing or pillarboxing the image.

 ✔ **Crop:** Click this button to display the green cropping box shown in Figure 7-5. Drag the corner handles to encompass the desired rectangle. iMovie keeps the rectangle's aspect ratio the same as the project's aspect ratio. Click inside the cropping box and drag to reposition it within the frame.

Figure 7-4:
The Viewer
buttons
when you're
cropping,
rotating, or
applying the
Ken Burns
Effect.

Figure 7-5:
You're ready
to crop
your clip.

✔ **Ken Burns:** Use this to set start and end rectangles for the Ken Burns Effect, as discussed later in this chapter.

✔ **Rotate counterclockwise:** Rotate the image 90 degrees to the left.

✔ **Rotate clockwise:** Rotate the image 90 degrees to the right.

✔ **Play clip:** Does just what the name says.

✔ **Done:** Click this button when you're finished with your editing task to accept the changes you've made.

Pressing Return or Enter is equivalent to clicking Done. Pressing Esc exits the tool, leaving things as they were before you selected it.

In a number of situations, you'll find that you need to combine two or more of the capabilities this tool offers to achieve your desired presentation. For example, you have a portrait image that you haven't yet rotated in iPhoto, so it's still "laying on its side." You also need to crop the image. You should proceed as follows:

1. **Rotate the photo so that it is right-side up.**

2. **Click the Fit button so that the whole image is presented in the frame and the default Ken Burns Effect is no longer in effect.**

   You will find the image is now pillarboxed (has black bars at the left and right of the image).

3. **Click the Crop button to display the cropping rectangle.**

4. **Drag the rectangle up or down so that it encloses the vertical portion of your photo that you want displayed.**

5. **(optional) Drag the cropping rectangle's corners to hone in on an even smaller portion of the image.**

Make certain that you leave enough pixels for your intended distribution medium. For example, if you're targeting HDTV, iMovie prefers a resolution of at least 1920×1080; however, if your target is an iPod, 320×240 should suffice. You could crop to a smaller selection, but then iMovie has to scale the image up to fit your viewing frame. Scaling up video, just like scaling up images in iPhoto, often results in jagged or blurry video.

Applying the Ken Burns Effect

When Steve Jobs presented the first public demonstration of iMovie 3 at San Francisco's 2003 Macworld Expo, the feature producing the greatest positive reaction was the Ken Burns Effect, a pan-and-zoom technique that actually predated Mr. Burns. Mr. Jobs most likely named it after Ken Burns due to Burns' avid use of the technique in his PBS documentaries. We're going to call it the *KBE*, at least during this discussion, to avoid wasting space by writing it out every time.

The KBE is used to give life, or, in other words, motion, to still images. The process involves selecting a starting rectangle and an ending rectangle within an image. The effect then pans and zooms to move from having the starting rectangle fill the screen to having the ending rectangle fill the screen. In most respects, it is analogous to the morphing of one shape into another, where you view the progress through intermediate shapes, and the KBE shows you the progress from one vantage point and visual focus to another. A couple of ways you can use the KBE are

- **Zoom in or zoom out:** To zoom in, set a large starting rectangle and a much smaller enclosed rectangle (generally centered within the large rectangle), as shown in Figure 7-6. Reverse the rectangles for a zoom-out effect. The starting rectangle is green and the ending rectangle is red.

✏ **Pan across a row of people:** Just because you're working with a still image doesn't mean that you can't make your audience believe that you shot a clip panning across a group. Place your starting rectangle around the left end of the row and your ending rectangle around the right end for a left-to-right pan, as shown in Figure 7-7. Notice the helpful yellow arrow that iMovie displays, showing the motion's direction.

iMovie places a few restrictions on the use of the KBE, the most notable being that the starting and ending rectangles must overlap on a left-to-right pan due to limitations on how small the rectangles are allowed to be. This means, for example, in the case of panning across a scene, that you can't focus in too tightly. The result is that you can't pan across the group one face at a time (unless the group is only two people).

Make use of the Play Clip button at the top of the Viewer to test your effect. If things aren't quite right, adjust one or both rectangles and preview the clip again. Keep tweaking the rectangles until you have the best result available.

Combine the KBE with an opening freeze frame and you'll come close to reproducing the scene openers in Donald Bellasario's very popular *NCIS* television series.

Figure 7-6:
Time to
zoom in on
the little red
wagon.

Figure 7-7:
Pan across
a row of
people to
give the
illusion
of motion
video.

Adjusting Duration

By default, iMovie gives all still clips a four-second duration. Those of you who used versions of iMovie prior to iMovie '08 might wonder why the default was changed from five seconds to four seconds. We wondered, too, but couldn't get a response other than "Lots of users complained that five seconds was too long, but it doesn't really matter — you can always set your own default for a project." We can't really find fault with that answer because one size doesn't fit all and we do change the duration on almost a still-by-still basis. We tend to slow down long pans or zooms by making the duration longer and speed up any opening and closing freeze frames by shortening their durations. So, if you want a different default duration in your project, choose File➪Project Properties, click the Timing tab, and set the photo duration you prefer.

Here's how to adjust a still clip's duration:

1. **Select the clip in the Project pane.**

2. **Open the Clip Inspector by double-clicking the clip, clicking the Inspector button in the toolbar, choosing Window➪Clip Adjustments, or pressing I.**

   The Clip Inspector opens, as shown in Figure 7-8.

3. **Type your new duration in the Duration text box.**

   Remember that the duration you type should reflect the time display you've chosen. In other words, to get a 5 second duration, type **5** if your display is set up to show hh:mm:ss, but type **5:00** if it's displaying hh:mm:ss:frames.

4. **(Optional.) To change the durations of all stills in your project (and set a default for all new still clips), select the Applies to All Stills check box.**

Figure 7-8:
The Clip
Inspector
with a
still clip
selected.

 Because selecting Applies to All Stills changes the durations of all existing stills, we recommend placing any stills you have that are going to obey the default duration first, and *then* deselecting the Applies to All Stills check box before placing and setting durations for any still clips that differ in duration.

8

Using Themes to Enhance Your Movie

In This Chapter

▷ Exploring the available themes

▷ Picking a theme

▷ Working with themes

▷ Animating travel maps

A s fourteenth-century filmmaker Geoffrey Chaucer once said after a long session in the editing room, "The lyf so short, the craft so long to lerne." And it *can* take a long time to learn the craft of editing a movie.

That's where iMovie themes come in. Themes provide your movie with opening and closing titles, provide specially designed transitions, and give your work a coherent visual design.

Understanding iMovie Themes

When you create a new project, you choose a theme for the project, as you saw in Chapter 5. To refresh your memory, Figure 8-1 shows you the New Project dialog again.

© iStockphoto/Steve Mann

When we showed this dialog to you last time, we glossed over the most important part of it, at least as far as the amount of screen space it takes up: that group of six labeled squares in the center of the dialog that represent the available project themes.

As you can see in Figure 8-1, the default theme is no theme at all. If you have been playing around in iMovie as you've read through this book, that's the theme you've most likely been using. But just what is a theme?

Figure 8-1:
The New
Project
dialog:
You've seen
it before.

A *theme* is a template for the look of your movie. It includes an opening title, a set of customized transitions, a closing title, and a generalized recipe for combining and applying those elements to a movie.

For example, Figure 8-2 shows a very simple five-clip movie project that uses the None theme. Figure 8-3 shows the same project with the Comic Book theme applied.

Notice the colored bars above the clips at the beginning and the end of the themed movie, and the little squares between the clips that comprise the movie. The bars are title overlays and the squares are transitions.

Figure 8-2:
A simple
project with
the None
theme.

Figure 8-3:
The same
simple
project with
the Comic
Book theme.

You find out more — much more — about titles and transitions in Chapter 9, but here's the short take:

- ✓ **Theme titles**: These insert video of the opening and closing clips into animated graphic frames. The graphic frames include text labels. A theme's opening title by default displays the name of the project as the movie's title. The closing title by default displays a director's credit that uses the user name for the Mac OS X account in which iMovie is running, as shown in Figure 8-4. You can change the text if you want; see Chapter 9 for how to edit the text of an iMovie title.

- ✓ **Transitions:** These provide a gradual visual shift between two adjacent clips rather than having the video image shift abruptly from one clip to the next. The lack of transition is called a *jump cut.*

The transitions that a theme provides come in two varieties:

- ✓ **Standard cross-dissolve transitions:** Cross-dissolves blend two clips together, so that final frames of one clip are overlaid on the opening frames of the next clip. As the transition plays, the frames of the first clip become more transparent while the frames of the next clip become more opaque. Unless you override iMovie's default settings, the theme that you have selected controls how long the transition lasts — usually about half a second. Figure 8-5 shows a cross-dissolve midway through the transition.

- ✓ **Theme-styled transitions:** This transition selects individual frames from your movie and inserts them into an animated graphic that plays between the two clips. By default, theme-styled transitions usually take a couple of seconds to play. Figure 8-6 shows a theme-styled transition in the Comic Book theme. In the section, "Customizing Transitions in a Themed Project" later in this chapter, we explain how to select which frames in your movie are used in a theme-styled transition.

Figure 8-4:
A closing
title in the
Comic Book
theme.

Figure 8-5:
A cross-
dissolve
transition in
progress.

Figure 8-6:
A Comic
Book
theme-
styled
transition in
progress.

When you choose a theme, you specify whether iMovie adds automatic transitions to your movie. If you choose automatic transitions, you cannot edit them or add additional transitions to your movie. iMovie handles the transitions for you completely: That's why they're called "automatic." Of course, you can turn off automatic transitions at any time and then edit those that have been added after you do.

In addition to the None theme, here are the five themes that iMovie '09 supplies:

- Photo Album
- Bulletin Board
- Comic Book
- Scrapbook
- Filmstrip

You can choose a theme when you create a project, or at any time while you are working on a project. And after you have chosen a theme, you are not wedded to it: You can change a movie's theme at any time.

When you see a Themes dialog, such as the one shown in Figure 8-1, you can put your pointer over each theme thumbnail to get a preview of the theme's visual style.

Applying Themes

You can add a theme to a project or change the current theme at any time. You can change a theme in any one of these ways:

- Choose File ➪ Project Properties (⌘+J).
- Right-click in the project pane and choose Project Properties.
- Click Set Theme in the Titles pane of the Media Browser.
- Click Set Theme in the Transitions pane of the Media Browser (see Figure 8-7).

When you choose Project Properties, the theme selection choices are included in the dialog with other project properties you can set, as shown in Figure 8-8.

When you apply a theme to an existing project that has the default None theme, the Automatically Add Transitions and Titles check box presents you with some choices when you select it.

Figure 8-7:
The
Transitions
pane of
the Media
Browser
gives you
theme
control.

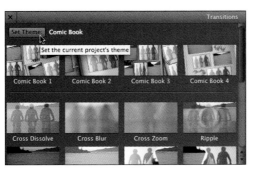

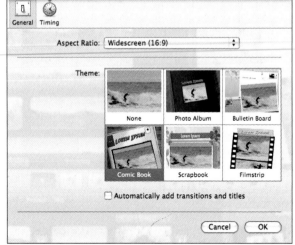

Figure 8-8:
The Project
Properties
dialog
includes
theme
choices.

Figure 8-9 shows the choices you have when you change from the default None theme to another theme and select the Automatically Add Transitions and Titles check box. You see a similar dialog whenever you change themes in a project that has clips without transitions and you choose to add automatic transitions.

Because the cross-dissolve transitions used in themes make use of the frames of two adjacent clips simultaneously, your movie becomes shorter by the duration of each cross-dissolve. That's the default choice: Overlap Ends and Shorten Clip is selected.

Figure 8-9:
This dialog
appears
when you
add a theme
to a project
and
automa-
tically add
transitions
and titles.

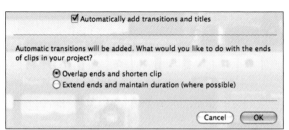

If you don't want your movie to become shorter when you add a theme and choose automatic transitions and titles, however, iMovie can try to use footage from beyond the ends of adjacent clips in your movie for the transitions. That's what the second choice, Extend Ends and Maintain Duration (Where Possible), does. Of course, if you use an entire source clip in your movie, iMovie won't be able to extend that clip's duration, which is why iMovie adds the (Where Possible) codicil to the second choice.

Changing Themes

When your project has a theme (other than None) and you change the project's theme, you can tell iMovie what to do with the titles and transitions it has already added.

When you change your project's theme from one theme to another, and you continue to automatically add transitions and titles, you don't need to make any other choices. iMovie automatically changes the theme transitions and titles to those used in the new theme. It's like having a house redecorated: the rooms and hallways remain exactly where they always were, but the furnishings, paint, wallpaper, and carpet change.

iMovie gives you the choices shown in Figure 8-10 if you deselect the Automatically Add Transitions and Titles check box.

Figure 8-10: Your choices when you decide not to automatically add titles and transitions.

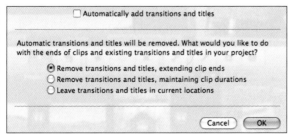

The choices are reasonably straightforward:

✓ **Remove Transitions and Titles, Extending Clip Ends:** You can have iMovie strip all transitions and titles from your movie and restore the clips in your project to their original lengths. You can still add theme titles and transitions manually to the project.

✔ **Remove Transition and Titles, Maintaining Clip Durations:** You can have iMovie strip the transitions and titles, but leave the clips in the project shortened by the amount they were made when the transitions were added originally. You might want to choose this option, for example, if you have overlaid audio that will be affected by a change in the movie's length.

✔ **Leave Transitions and Titles in Current Locations:** You can leave everything that the theme added or changed intact. This means that your movie still has the theme's look and feel, for the most part, but you are free to use other transitions and title styles in your movie as you continue to work. You can also modify the transitions and titles that the theme adds.

But what happens to your project if you change to the None theme from one of the other themes (in essence, remove the theme)? There are two possibilities:

✔ You can select the Automatically Add check box and choose a transition from the pop-up menu. This strips all the theme-based titles from your movie and puts the selected transition between each of your clips.

✔ You can deselect the Automatically Add check box. In that case, the theme-based titles are all removed, but you can make a choice about what to do with the transitions that iMovie has previously added to your project, as shown in Figure 8-11.

The first two choices are pretty self-explanatory. The third choice, however, has some subtle implications. It doesn't, in fact, leave any of the theme-based transitions in your project — those get stripped out. But it *does* leave any cross-dissolve transitions already in place.

Figure 8-11:
When you de-theme a project, you can make some choices.

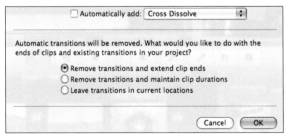

☐ Automatically add: Cross Dissolve

Automatic transitions will be removed. What would you like to do with the ends of clips and existing transitions in your project?

⦿ Remove transitions and extend clip ends
◯ Remove transitions and maintain clip durations
◯ Leave transitions in current locations

Cancel   OK

Customizing Themes

How much you can customize a theme depends on whether you have set it to automatically add titles and transitions.

In the case where you are running on automatic, as it were, you can add titles to any clip that doesn't already have a title attached to it, and you can change the durations and frames used in the transitions that iMovie has put in place. Here's what you *can't* do:

- ✓ Change or remove the titles that iMovie has placed automatically
- ✓ Remove the transitions that iMovie has added automatically
- ✓ Add additional transitions

Adding Titles to a Themed Project

Chapter 9 describes the care and feeding of titles in detail, but here are the basics for adding titles to a themed movie that has automatic titles and transitions turned on.

1. **In the toolbar, click the Title button to see the available titles in the Media Browser.**

   In addition to the title styles that iMovie makes available for all projects, a set of theme-related title thumbnails appears at the top of the Media Browser.

2. **Drag a title thumbnail over a clip in your project that doesn't have a title.**

   If you drag the title thumbnail over the beginning or the end of the clip, the first third or last third of the clip is highlighted, as shown in Figure 8-12. If you drag the title thumbnail over the center of the clip, the entire clip is highlighted. When you drop the title thumbnail, the title appears over the section of the clip that was highlighted.

3. **In the Viewer, click on the title text and change it to your liking, as shown in Figure 8-13, and then click Done.**

Figure 8-12:
Where you drop the title on a clip affects the title's duration.

Figure 8-13:
See a title;
change a
title.

Customizing Transitions in a Themed Project

Although automatic titles and transitions in a themed project prohibit you from removing or adding transitions to the project, you still can adjust the transitions that the theme has placed in the project.

You can make the following kinds of changes to transitions in a themed project that has automatic transitions enabled:

- Change which frames are displayed in a theme-styled transition
- Change transition duration
- Control the type of transition (non-theme-styled only)

As you saw back in Figure 8-6, a theme-styled transition uses individual frames drawn from your movie project as part of the transition graphic. To choose different frames for the transition graphic, click the theme-styled transition icon between two clips. When you do, the project pane shows you from where the frames used in the transition are drawn, as seen in Figure 8-14.

Figure 8-14:
Pointers
show where
a theme-
styled
transition
gets its
images.

The numbers in the project pane correspond to those shown in the Viewer pane, as seen in Figure 8-15.

Figure 8-15: The transition graphic frames are numbered in the viewer.

Here's how you change a frame used in the transition graphic:

1. **Drag the pointer in the project pane to a different location in the project.**

   The transition graphic shown in the viewer pane adjusts itself.

2. **In the viewer pane, click Done.**

To adjust the transition duration and, for non-theme-styled transitions, the type of transition, do the following:

1. **Position the playhead over the transition icon, click the action button that appears below it, and then choose Transition Adjustments from the action menu that appears, as shown in Figure 8-16.**

   We discuss the Transitions Adjustments menu again in Chapter 9.

2. **In the Inspector, change the duration and select whether the change applies only to the current transition or to all transitions in the project, as shown in Figure 8-17.**

Figure 8-16: The action menu for transitions.

Figure 8-17:
The
transition
Inspector.

3. **For non-theme-styled transitions, click the transition type, and then, when the Inspector rotates to show you the available transition choices, click a transition style.**

   iMovie applies the transition style you clicked, and the Inspector rotates back to show its face again.

4. **In the Inspector, click Done.**

Going to Manual transitions

Automatic transitions and titles can take a lot of the work out of building an iMovie project. All you have to do is choose the clips and the order in which they appear, and iMovie links them all together in an attractive presentation. However, you don't have to be hamstrung completely by iMovie's automatic decisions. You can keep the theme, but wrest control of when, where, and how titles and transitions appear.

Getting manual control of your titles and transitions is almost absurdly simple: Just try to do something that iMovie doesn't want you to do. That is, drag a title thumbnail over an iMovie-generated title bar, or drag a different transition over an iMovie-generated transition. When you commit this heinous crime, iMovie displays the dialog shown in Figure 8-18.

All you have to do is click Turn Off Automatic Transitions. Of course, after you do that, iMovie no longer generates transitions and titles for you when you add clips to your project. You're on your own: master of your own destiny. Don't turn automatic transitions back on, though, or you'll lose your customizations.

Figure 8-18:
Use this
dialog to
regain title
and transi-
tion control
in a themed
project.

Applying an Animated Travel Map

Okay, we admit it: This section really has nothing to do with themes, but there's really no other good place for it to go in this book, and it somehow thematically *feels* as if it belongs with iMovie themes. So we're putting it here.

Just as iMovie's themes give you graphically sophisticated animated titles and transitions, iMovie can also give you animated maps that you can use to enhance your projects. Maps provide visually interesting introductions to scenes in movies that take place in various locations around the world. (Sorry, iMovie offers no extraterrestrial maps — at this time.)

You can insert maps between clips in your project to let the audience know where the next sequence takes place, and you can even show the course of a journey *Indiana Jones*-style, where a line is drawn on the map indicating the journey's path. And you can choose from a variety of map styles that can harmonize with the theme you may have chosen for your project.

 To get access to the iMovie map collection, click the Maps and Backgrounds button at the far right of the toolbar. The Media Browser presents its maps and backgrounds, with the eight animated maps and four still maps at the top. They come in four styles, and each style comes in both a globe and a flat animated version and in a still flat version (see Figure 8-19):

- ✓ Old World
- ✓ Watercolor
- ✓ Educational
- ✓ Blue Marble

 You can use both animated maps and still maps as the background for movie titles. See Chapter 9 for more about titles and backgrounds.

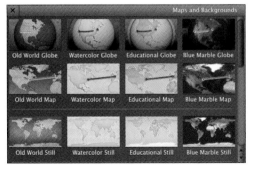

Figure 8-19: Maps that move and maps that don't.

To use an animated map, just drag its thumbnail from the Media Browser to your project and drop it on a clip: Drop it near the beginning of the clip to have the map precede the clip, and drop it near the end of a clip to have the map follow the clip.

If your project uses a theme with automatic transitions and titles, iMovie adds a transition before or after the map just as it would for any other clip that you add to the project.

When you add an animated map to your project, iMovie presents its Map Inspector, as seen in Figure 8-20. You use the Inspector to do the following:

- Set the duration of the animation
- Apply one of iMovie's standard video effects to the map
- Set the location where the map animation begins
- Optionally, set the location where the animation ends

If you do not set an end location for the animated map, the animation centers on the start location and animates the location's label on the map.

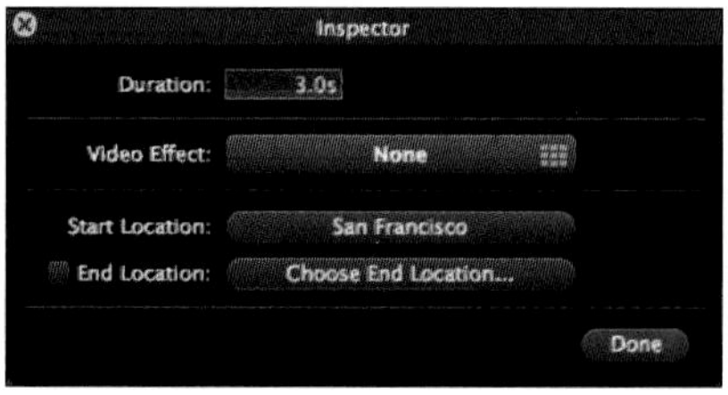

Figure 8-20:
The Map
Inspector.

Here's how to set a location:

1. **Click Start Location or End Location.**

   The Inspector rotates to display the Choose City or Airport dialog.

2. **Enter a city, state, country, or airport code in the search field.**

   iMovie offers possible matching locations from its database of locations, as shown in Figure 8-21.

3. **Click a location.**

   iMovie places it in the dialog's Name to Display on Map field.

Figure 8-21:
Choose a
location
from
iMovie's
geographic
database.

4. If necessary, edit the display name.

If you can only find a location near the one you want, choose it and
change the display name. The map is not so accurate that your audience
can tell the difference between, say, Malibu (in the database) and Pacific
Palisades (not in the database) in Southern California.

5. Click OK.

The dialog rotates back to the Map Inspector.

When you have both a start and end location specified, the Map Inspector
offers you a control that you can use to swap the two locations, so that the
end becomes the start and vice versa, as shown in Figure 8-22. The Inspector
also shows the distance between the two locations.

Click Done to close the Map Inspector and play the animated map clip to see
your travel map in action.

Swap start and end locations.

Figure 8-22:
Swap start
and end
locations
with the
curvy arrow
button in
the Map
Inspector.

Part III
In the Cutting Room

The 5th Wave   By Rich Tennant

RICHTENNANT

THE LEVINES EDIT THEIR AFRICAN SAFARI VIDEO

"Do you think the 'Hidden Rhino' clip should come before or after the 'Waving Hello' video clip?"

© iStockphoto/PHi2

In this part . . .

In these chapters, we cover the following topics:

- ✔ Chapter 9 shows you how to add titles, subtitles, and captions. It also explains how to add transitions between clips, and how to add video effects, such as a sepia tone, to clips in your movie.

- ✔ Chapter 10 shows you how to use iMovie's Precision Editor to make precise and complex edits to your movie's clips.

- ✔ Chapter 11 surveys iMovie's audio editing capabilities.

9

Adding Titles, Transitions, and Effects

In This Chapter

▷ Adding titles and text frames

▷ Transitioning between clips

▷ Employing visual effects

---

*N*o matter how wonderful your footage or how compelling your movie's message, you still want to introduce your opus in the best possible manner. The textual introduction of your movie's title, possible text effects to set various scenes, the visual segue from one scene to the next, and visual effects to set or enhance a mood are all post-production activities that have stood the test of time. iMovie provides you with all these capabilities in its customary easy-to-use way. In this chapter, we show you what you can do with titles, transitions, and visual effects, and how to do it.

Working with Titles

The word *titles* is such an unassuming term to cover the broad range of textual adornment iMovie provides. Whether you're looking for a static white-on-black title still, rolling credits, or scene captioning, iMovie provides you with a wealth of textual effects from which to choose.

©iStockphoto/cb43inc

Picking a title type

T You access iMovie's one-stop title shopping emporium via the Show or Hide Title Browser button in the iMovie toolbar, shown in the margin, by choosing Window⇨Titles, or pressing ⌘+3. Our preference is to press ⌘+3 when we're using the keyboard or to click the Title Browser button when driving the mouse/trackball/trackpad.

When you display the Title Browser, you see something similar to Figure 9-1 (the selection of titles varies, depending upon the Theme you're using in your project). Thirty-two title presentations are always available, and they're the only ones you see when your Theme choice is None. Theme-specific titles appear at the top of the scrolling thumbnail array, separated from the ubiquitous titles by a thin horizontal line, as shown in Figure 9-2.

You can change themes freely right from the Title Browser. Just click the Set Theme button at the upper left to display the Theme Picker dialog and make your choice. The current theme's name is displayed to the right of the Set Theme button.

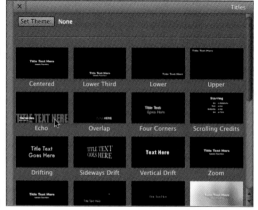

Figure 9-1:
The Title
Browser
displays
thumbnails
of the titles
available to
your proj-
ect's theme.

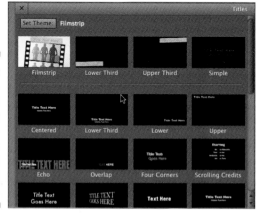

Figure 9-2:
A hori-
zontal line
separates
Theme-
specific
titles from
regular title
choices.

Table 9-1 is a rundown of the titles available to all projects, with a very brief overview of each:

Table 9-1	Title Styles for All Themes	
Thumbnail	*Name*	*Brief Description*
	Centered	Static, two-line title centered on the screen, the top line being the title in large type and the bottom line being an optional subtitle.
	Lower Third	The same as Centered, but with the text positioned in the bottom third of the screen.
	Lower	One line of title text, in the bottom-right corner of the screen.
	Upper	One line of title text, in the upper-left screen corner.
	Echo	A line of title text above a smaller line of subtitle text in the bottom-left corner of the screen, with the title text line repeated in a neutral gray (all caps) across the bottom of the screen. If the title is too long to fit initially, the characters are made narrower to make it fit.

(continued)

Table 9-1 *(continued)*

Thumbnail	Name	Brief Description
	**Overlap**	This title style is animated. By default, the title is in red and moves into the frame from the left; the subtitle is in white and moves in from the right. After pausing in place, they move offscreen in the same directions as they entered, overlapping as they pass (hence the name).
	**Four Corners**	Another animated style, the title comes into the frame from the left center and stops, whereas the subtitle enters the frame from the bottom, stopping just below the title. Then, they do a slight Ken Burns Effect zoom in, followed by the title moving offscreen at the top-right corner and the subtitle moving out-of-frame at the right.
	**Scrolling Credits**	This title style should be familiar to anyone who's ever stayed for a movie's closing credits. A header (the default is "Starring") is followed by line after line of two text columns, with the performer's name in the left column and the role in the right column. You replace the four placeholders with your own credits, but when it comes to adding additional rows, there is a small trick that isn't that obvious: press Return to create a new row and then press Tab to position the cursor to where the right end of the name would be. Press Tab again to position to the start of the second column. Repeat as necessary for additional lines.

Thumbnail	Name	Brief Description
	Drifting	An animated two-row title where the top line comes to the center rapidly from the left, hovers briefly, and then exits rapidly to the right. The second line does the same zip-hover-zip sequence, but from the opposite direction.
	Sideways Drift	Very similar to Drifting, but with a perspective effect where the characters increase in size from left to right, giving the impression that the top line is coming toward you and the bottom line is receding in the distance.
	Vertical Drift	Similar to Drifting, but with the left half of the line coming in from the screen bottom and zipping off the top; the right half of the line whips in from the top, hovers and speeds off the bottom.
	Zoom	The same layout as Centered, but the text fades into the center, gradually zooming in some more, then fading out.
	Horizontal Blur	The text emerges from blurred horizontal stripes, zooms in slightly, and then dissolves back into blurred horizontal stripes.
	Soft Edge	A single title line about two-thirds down from the top of the screen that softly fades into view, moves slowly toward the right, and then fades out of view.

(continued)

Table 9-1 *(continued)*

Thumbnail	Name	Brief Description
	Lens Flare	Lens flares cross and the title line appears in the center of the screen, sits there, and then fades out. This title effect does not allow specifying a different font, as we discuss later in this chapter.
	Pull Focus	Similar to Centered, except that the text fades in and fades out, with the characters having a thin black outline.
	Boogie Lights	Flashing lights, text fades into the center, and then flashing lights again.
	Pixie Dust	Like Boogie Lights, but with the flashing lights replaced with sparkling pixie dust, a la Disney's Tinkerbell.
	Organic Main	An ornate, script title with a decorative vine-like accent to the upper-left and lower-right fades into view, hovers in the center of the screen, and then fades out. This title effect does not allow you to specify a different font.
	Organic Lower	The text and vine-like accents fade in over a parchment stripe at the bottom of the screen. You cannot choose a different font for this title effect.

Thumbnail	Name	Brief Description
	Ticker	Your title marches from left to right along the bottom of the screen in a manner similar to a stock market ticker tape. You may not specify a different font for this title style.
	Date/Time	This effect places the time and date your project was created in the bottom-left corner of the screen. You have no control over any aspect of the Date/Time title style.
	Clouds	Blue (left) and pink (right) clouds bounce out of the bottom of the screen and settle there, displaying your title text. You do not have control over the font used in this effect.
	Far, Far Away	This is the familiar *Star Wars* opening effect, where line after line of text comes in from the bottom of the screen and narrows as it scrolls up, giving the effect of fading into the distance. You can have as many lines of text as you wish.
	Gradient — White	A title line and a subtitle line centered in a white-to-transparent radial gradient stripe along the bottom of the screen. The stripe and text fade in quickly, sit there, and then fade out quickly at the end of the clip.
	Soft Bar — White	Similar to Gradient — White, but with a solid white bar rather than a gradient.

(continued)

Table 9-1 *(continued)*

Thumbnail	Name	Brief Description
	Paper	Similar to Gradient — White, but with a frayed-edge paper background in place of the gradient stripe.
	Formal	Similar to Soft Bar — White, but with a little screen space below the white bar.
	Gradient — Black	A black-to-transparent linear gradient background along the bottom of the screen with the text left-justified.
	Soft Bar — Black	White text at the left edge of a black bar across the bottom of the screen.
	Torn Edge — Black	Imagine frayed, black construction paper, with the text at the right end laid across the bottom of the screen and you'll recognize this style.
	Torn Edge — Tan	This is Torn Edge — Black, with tan in place of black.

To add a title to your project, click the title style you want to use and drag it to your project, into the position you want it. Note that you can place it between clips or have it play over a clip. We explain how in the next two sections.

Adding a title over a clip

To have your video play over existing footage, proceed as follows:

1. **Drag the title style you want to use to your project, letting it hover over a clip.**

   A purple highlight appears, indicating the frames on which the title appears.

2. **Release the mouse button.**

   A blue title bar appears over the frames where the title plays, as shown in Figure 9-3.

3. **(Optional.) If you want a different duration, double-click the blue bar to present the Inspector, as shown in Figure 9-4.**

   Adjust the duration as desired. Alternatively, you can drag the blue bar until the desired duration appears.

Figure 9-3:
A blue bar shows your title text, the duration, and which frames it covers.

Figure 9-4:
The Inspector lets you change a title's duration, style, and the fade in/out lengths.

4. **Select the blue bar.**

   The title editor appears in the Viewer, as shown in Figure 9-5.

5. **Select the text placeholders and replace them with your text.**

6. **(Optional.) If the Show Fonts button is present and you wish to use a different typeface, click the Show Fonts button.**

   The iMovie Fonts Panel, shown in Figure 9-6, appears. The nine iMovie fonts are in the left column, the nine color options in the second column, and the nine available sizes in the right column. Select a style (Bold, Italic, or Outlined) if desired from the style buttons below the list and an alignment choice from the Alignment buttons (left justified, centered, fully justified, and right justified). If you want more font flexibility, click the System Font Panel button and the window flips over to present the standard Mac OS X Font panel.

7. **(Optional, but recommended.) Click the Play button in the Viewer to preview your title.**

8. **Click Done to exit the title editor.**

Figure 9-5:
Customize
and preview
your title in
the Viewer's
title editor
display.

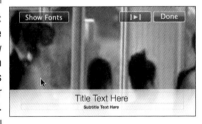

Figure 9-6:
The iMovie
Font Panel
displays the
iMovie fonts
and the
available
colors and
sizes.

The iMovie Font Panel, described in Step 6, is a little bit like a menu in a Chinese restaurant: pick one from column A, one from column B, and one from column C. For example, you could select a pale blue Futura Medium in size 9 (and no, that's not point size, but just a 1–9 scale of increasing sizes) or a size 2 black Coolvetica or any of the other 727 combinations.

In addition to being useful as actual titles and credits, titles applied over clips are useful for captioning: We've even seen them used to present lyrics for sing-along purposes. It's not quite karaoke, but it's a reasonable facsimile.

Adding titles between clips

If you don't want your titles appearing over your footage, proceed as follows:

1. **Select the title you want to use and drag it to the beginning of your project (common for an opening title), the end of project (often used for closing credits), or between clips (usually used to set up a scene).**

    The Choose Background panel appears, as shown in Figure 9-7. As you hover the mouse pointer over a background, you see a preview in the Viewer.

2. **Click the background of choice and iMovie places it in your project at the point selected in Step 1, as shown in Figure 9-8.**

    A blue title bar appears over the clip, listing the duration and text (or at least the beginning thereof).

3. **With the blue title bar selected, replace the placeholder text with your text in the Viewer.**

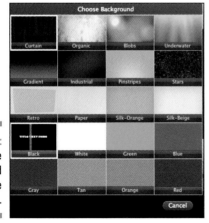

Figure 9-7: Choose the background for your title clip here.

Figure 9-8:
iMovie
places your
clip with the
selected
background
in your
project.

4. **If you wish to use a different font, size, and/or color and the Show Fonts button is present, which indicates that you may customize the fonts, click the Show Fonts button to display the iMovie Font Panel, shown previously in Figure 9-6.**

   Using the iMovie Font Panel is described in the previous section of this chapter.

5. **If you wish to change the duration, any fade in/out timing, or even the title style, double-click the blue title bar to display the Inspector, shown previously in Figure 9-4, and make your adjustments.**

6. **Click Done in the Viewer to exit from title editing mode.**

Some ways you might employ titles between clips include

✓ Introducing a scene or sequence in your movie: for example, "Day 2, Kauai" in a vacation video about your week in the Aloha State.

✓ Providing expository text about products in a catalog video.

✓ Providing dialogue when simulating a silent film.

In the iMovie Font Panel, mentioned in Step 4, you have to pick one from column A, one from column B, and one from column C. This gives you 729 possible combinations (9×9×9) of font, size, and color, without even considering stylistic variations (bold, italic, and outlined).

Employing Transitions

As described in Chapter 8, iMovie's themes include professionally selected transitions that are placed between clips. You can select your own transitions, in those cases where you don't grant iMovie's themes dictatorial control, in the Transitions Browser. To show the Transitions Browser, do one of the following:

↝ Click the Show or Hide Transitions browser button in the iMovie toolbar.

↝ Choose Window⇨Transitions.

↝ Press ⌘+4.

iMovie provides 20 transitions regardless of the theme in use. Each theme has its own set of transitions, whose names consist of the theme name and a number, as shown in the top row of thumbnails in Figure 9-9, in addition to the ubiquitous 20.

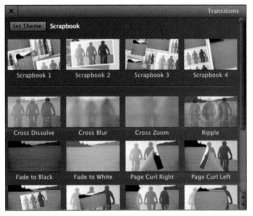

Figure 9-9: Theme-specific transitions are grouped together in the Transitions browser.

The ever-present 20 transitions are

↝ **Cross Dissolve:** Probably the most classic transition, the cross dissolve overlays the ends of the adjacent clips, fading out the frames from the clip that is ending while fading in the frames from the new clip.

↝ **Cross Blur:** Very similar to the Cross Dissolve, Cross Blur blurs the frames from the clip that is ending while making the frames from the clip that is starting more distinct.

↝ **Cross Zoom:** Yet another variation on the previous transitions, Cross Zoom zooms out from the first clip and zooms in the second clip.

↝ **Ripple:** Ripple gives the appearance of ripples on water as the first clip gives way to the second.

↝ **Fade to Black:** The first clip fades out to a black background and the second clip fades into view.

↝ **Fade to White:** Like Fade to Black, but with a white background.

- **Page Curl Right:** The second clip appears incrementally from the top-left toward the bottom-right as a curling page effect takes place.

- **Page Curl Left:** From the top-right toward the bottom-left.

- **Spin In:** The second clip starts as a small centered rectangle tilted about 45 degrees, and then spins clockwise and grows to fill the screen.

- **Spin Out:** The first clip shrinks while spinning counter-clockwise to reveal the second clip.

- **Circle Open:** A circle in the center of the screen grows to fill the screen while revealing the second clip.

- **Circle Close:** The first clip disappears from view as a circle shrinks to nothing in the center of the screen.

- **Doorway:** A rectangle grows laterally to reveal the second clip.

- **Swap:** The first clip shrinks to a rectangle on the left and a rectangle on the right grows to fill the screen with the second clip.

- **Cube:** Many of you have seen this one before. Mac OS X uses it to show a user switch. The first scene is on one face of the cube, the second scene on the next face to the right. The cube rotates to the left, hiding the first clip and displaying the second.

- **Mosaic:** The first clip breaks up into mosaic tiles, which then display second clip fragments that coalesce to display the second clip.

- **Wipe Left:** Another classic transition, the first clip disappears from right to left, just like dirt under a squeegee, with the second clip appearing in the wiped area.

- **Wipe Right:** Reverse directions on Wipe Left and you've got this transition.

- **Wipe Up:** We hope the name makes this transition obvious by now.

- **Wipe Down:** And this transition, as well.

Although it doesn't appear in the Transitions browser, there is one more transition to consider, and that is the lack of a transition. A straight cut from one clip to the next is called a *jump cut*. Jump cuts are commonly employed when moving from one camera angle to another in a single scene and transitions are generally employed to give a sense of passing time or change of scene.

Hovering the mouse over any of the thumbnails in the Transitions browser presents a preview of the transition, just like skimming footage in the Project or Events browser.

To insert a transition between two clips, drag a transition from the Transitions browser into the Project pane. iMovie displays a vertical green bar indicating where the transition is to be placed, as shown in Figure 9-10.

Figure 9-10: iMovie shows you where the transition will go if you release the mouse button.

 iMovie displays a transition indicator (shown in the margin) wherever a transition exists. Double-click the transition indicator to display the Inspector, as shown in Figure 9-11. You can also choose Transition Adjustments from the action (gear) menu that appears when the mouse pointer is on or near the transition indicator. You can change the transition's duration (the default is 14 frames) by typing a new value in the Duration text box. Additionally, you can select the Applies to All Transitions check box. But, most conveniently, you can replace the transition with another by clicking the Transition button, displaying your current transition's name to have the Inspector spin around and grow to show the Choose Transition panel, seen in Figure 9-12. Select a new transition or click Cancel to keep your current transition: Either action returns you to the Inspector.

Figure 9-11: The Transitions Inspector.

 We would be remiss if we didn't include some advice concerning transitions: Pick just a few to use in your movie and employ those few consistently. The more transitions you use in your movie, the more distracting your audience will find them. Transitions are meant to segue between two clips, not to be a noticeable part of your movie. Personally, we think that Spin In, Spin Out, Swap, Cube, and Mosaic should be reserved for special situations, such as a slideshow, and rarely used in a movie.

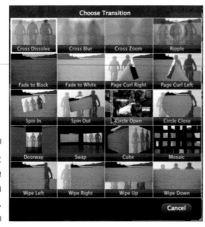

Figure 9-12:
The Choose
Transition
panel.

Applying Video Effects

We mentioned visual effects briefly in Chapter 6, with a promise to cover them more fully in this chapter, so here we go. Apple calls these *Video Effects* because you apply them to your video — the original iMovie product just called them Effects. Figure 9-13 shows the Choose Video Effect panel, which you access by clicking Video Effect button in the Clip Inspector.

The 20 available Video Effects are

- **None:** Enough said.
- **Flipped:** Everything on the left is now on the right, and vice versa. To the geometrically inclined, the image is reflected through the vertical axis.

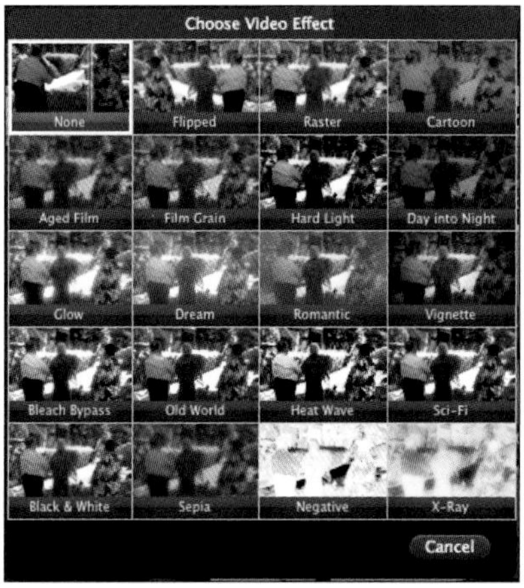

Figure 9-13:
Preview
and select
your Video
Effect in
the Choose
Video Effect
panel.

✔ **Raster:** The discrete pixels in the image are now evident, as though the frame is composed of a mass of small tiles.

✔ **Cartoon:** The number of colors is reduced, producing a more cartoonish feel to the video, hence the name.

✔ **Aged Film:** A sort of pebbled or crackled texture is applied, as though you used old film that was just starting to deteriorate.

✔ **Film Grain:** A fine, grainy texture is applied to your footage. The differences between Aged Film and Film Grain aren't always easy to discern.

✔ **Hard Light:** Familiar to Photoshop users, this is the video analog of the Hard Light blend mode. Imagine a harsh spotlight shining on your image — lighter colors get highlighted more and darker colors become starker.

✔ **Day into Night:** Everything gets darkened so that bright daylight scenes appear to be taken at twilight and nighttime footage looks almost midnight black, with dark shadows flitting across a darker backdrop.

✔ **Glow:** Intensifies the contrast.

✔ **Dream:** Adds a hazy overlay to your footage.

✔ **Romantic:** Adds an increasing haziness the closer you get to the edge of the frame, making the center of the frame stand out more.

✔ **Vignette:** An effect where the image's clarity degrades close to the edges or corners.

✔ **Bleach Bypass:** An effect where the whites look excessively bright, as if they had been bleached.

✔ **Old World:** Dulls the footage.

✔ **Heat Wave:** Adds a yellow cast to your footage, as though shot under a bright, hot sun.

✔ **Sci-Fi:** Washes out much of the color in your video.

✔ **Black & White:** Okay, this one should be obvious, right?

✔ **Sepia:** Adds a brown (sepia) tone to your footage, similar to the sepia-toned photos common in the early twentieth century and before.

✔ **Negative:** Inverts your footages colors, much like a photographic negative.

✔ **X-Ray:** Light and shadow against a black background, similar to an X-ray image (hence the name).

Double-click the desired Video Effect to select it or click Cancel to retain the current Effect. In either case, you return to the Clip Inspector.

TIP

Skimming over an effect's thumbnail presents a preview of the selected footage with that effect applied in the Viewer. Alternatively, you can press Space to have the preview repeat in a loop — while looping, you can move your mouse pointer to other effects to gauge the differences.

10

Precision Editing

In This Chapter

▷ Adding comment and chapter markers

▷ Fine-tuning a cut

▷ Editing video and audio separately

▷ Using greenscreen compositing

▷ Putting Picture in Picture in play

▷ Employing cutaways

Removing excess footage, stabilizing shaky video, and rearranging your clips are basic editing operations, and we cover those in Chapter 6. Adding titles and transitions and employing video effects are intermediate editing operations and we discussed those in Chapter 9. Themes and Maps were explored in Chapter 8.

In this chapter, we hit upon some advanced editing topics, most particularly a new iMovie feature that Apple has dubbed *precision editing*, hence this chapter's name. Precision editing also encompasses the use of some common video presentations, such as picture-in-picture and green-screen composition. We also discuss adding chapter markers to be used with iDVD and comment markers that serve as reminders while editing.

©iStockphoto/jerges cortina

Marking Frames

When you're browsing through your project's video, you invariably come across frames where you want to add a title, adjust the audio, or perform some other operation. You could stop each time you encounter such a frame, perform the desired operation, and then go back to browsing. We've tried that and found that we often got sidetracked, losing the browsing continuity as we went through the editing process. Similarly, when you're planning to put your opus on a DVD, you probably want to emulate professional movies and specify scenes that the viewer can jump to quickly.

iMovie helps you stay on track by providing *comment markers*, essentially video bookmarks where you tag a frame with a reminder so that you can go back and perform your editing at a more convenient time. To establish which frames a DVD viewer should be able to jump to, iMovie provides *chapter markers* as a cue to iDVD (see Chapter 15).

Setting a comment marker

We think you'll find that using comment markers makes your workflow smoother. Here's how to set a comment marker:

1. **Make sure that you have Advanced Tools turned on.**

   Choose iMovie⇨Preferences and select the Show Advanced Tools check box in the General pane if it isn't already selected.

2. **Drag a comment marker (see left margin) to the frame in your project.**

   A brown, numbered bar appears above your clip, centered on the frame you marked, as shown in Figure 10-1. Note that, if a comment marker is dragged to a frame of a title clip, rather than displaying a number, iMovie uses the title text as the marker's name.

3. **(Optional, but recommended.) Double-click the brown marker and type a reminder of why you marked this frame.**

   When you double-click the marker, the rectangle gets larger. Figure 10-2 shows the comment marker with a reminder that we want to make a freeze frame at this point. Notice that the marker resizes to accommodate the comment.

Figure 10-1:
A numbered marker above the frame.

Figure 10-2:
Type a
reminder
in your
comment
marker.

You can go back and edit a comment marker at any time by double-clicking the marker. You can also drag the comment marker to attach it to a different frame. To delete a comment marker, just click the brown marker to select it and press Delete.

Setting a chapter marker

When you purchase a commercial DVD and stick it into your DVD player, one of the first things you notice on most DVD menu screens, usually just below Play Movie, is a button with a name like Scene Selections or Chapter Selections. Using your DVD remote control to select the scene selection button displays a new screen with named or numbered images that let you pick where you want to start the movie playing. Your movies might not be as long or have as many scenes as a Hollywood blockbuster, but they often have sections that you really want to highlight. Consider the following examples:

- In your kid's Little League game, you might want to be able to jump directly to your little darling's at-bats or especially interesting plays in the field (whether a highlight or blooper).

- When viewing a school play, you might want to be able to go to a specific act or scene.

- For a recital or concert, you might want to be able to jump to specific musical numbers or to where particular performers come on-stage.

- In a vacation video, you might want to jump directly to a specific location (maybe the Painted Desert or the Grand Canyon on a trip through the American Southwest) or activity (for example, skiing, hang-gliding, cliff diving, or driving the bumper cars at Disneyland).

Just add chapter markers in iMovie. Then when you share your movie with iDVD, the Media Browser, or iTunes, or export it as a movie file in any size other than Tiny (sharing and exporting is covered in Chapter 12), your navigational aids are present for your viewers to take advantage of. To add a chapter marker, proceed as follows:

1. **Make sure that you have Advanced Tools turned on.**

   Choose iMovie⇨Preferences and select the Show Advanced Tools check box in the General pane if it isn't already selected.

2. **Drag a chapter marker (see left margin) to the frame in your project. An orange, numbered bar with an arrow appears above your clip, centered on the frame you marked, as shown in Figure 10-3.**

   "Orange" is the color Apple uses to describe it — it looks more like burnt sienna to us.

3. **(Optional, but recommended.) Double-click the orange marker and type a name for the chapter.**

   Your audience will find it easier to select a named scene than to remember (or try to figure out) what number goes with what scene, and you will, too. When you double-click the marker, the rectangle gets larger. Figure 10-4 shows the chapter marker with a (hopefully) recognizable name. Notice that the marker resizes to accommodate the chapter name.

TIP

Although it's not always the case, you'll discover that most of your chapter markers fall at the start of a scene. For that reason, you might want to avoid placing transitions at the clip boundaries where marked scenes begin, or at least avoid the more active transitions lest your audience jump into the middle of a transition, missing at least part of the desired effect.

Figure 10-3:
iMovie places a numbered orange marker above the frame you marked.

Figure 10-4:
Type a chapter name in your chapter marker.

Navigating a marked course

As your project fills with markers, you may begin to find that locating a specific marker becomes more and more difficult. Scanning the little orange and brown bars for a particular text string requires close attention, so Apple made it easy by adding a drop-down menu button next to the comment and chapter marker icons in the Project Browser's upper-right corner, as shown in Figure 10-5. A quick click and you have a menu of your markers, conveniently arranged to help you find what you seek.

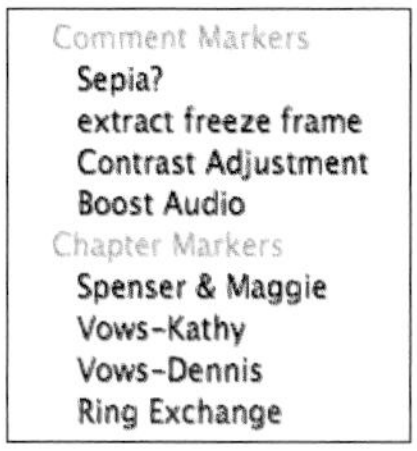

Figure 10-5:
Go directly
to your
marker by
choosing
it from the
marker
menu.

Comment Markers
 Sepia?
 extract freeze frame
 Contrast Adjustment
 Boost Audio
Chapter Markers
 Spenser & Maggie
 Vows–Kathy
 Vows–Dennis
 Ring Exchange

Editing Precisely

When you apply a transition, iMovie shortens the clips on either side of the transition when performing the blend. When viewing your footage normally, you don't see the excised frames. However, when using the precision editor, you see and can work with the unused frames on either side of the transition point, witnessing the effect your modifications have on the transition.

Editing a transition point

If you want to edit a transition between two clips, proceed as follows:

1. **Open the Precision Editor by choosing Precision Editor from the Action menu (see margin) that appears when you move the mouse pointer over the transition, as shown in Figure 10-6.**

   The Precision Editor opens in the space normally occupied by the Event Library and Event Browser, as shown in Figure 10-7.

   The frames at the left end of the top row are those that play before the transition, those at the right end of the bottom row are those that play after the transition, and the remaining (shaded) frames are those that are not currently used in your project. The transition appears as an icon between the top and bottom rows.

Figure 10-6:
Choose
Precision
Editor from
the Action
menu.

Figure 10-7:
The
Precision
Editor pane.

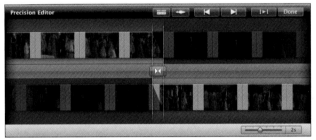

2. **To move the *cut point*, the frame where one clip ends and the next begins, just click the frame that you want to be the cut point (in either clip). The filmstrip slides to position the new frame at the cut point.**

   In this manner, you can manually adjust how many frames from either clip are subsumed by the transition. Figure 10-8 shows a Fade to White transition between an outdoor scene and an indoor scene. Figure 10-9 shows the result of sliding both filmstrips to the right, in effect fading more of the clip that is ending and concealing less of the clip that is starting. Be aware that sliding the cut points only moves the start and end points and doesn't alter the transition's duration.

3. **Click Done when finished to close the Precision Editor.**

You can also drag the end of either filmstrip to slide it until the desired frame is at the cut point.

Click the Extras button (see margin) to toggle whether indicators (icons, markers, titles, and so on) above the top filmstrip or below the bottom filmstrip are present, as shown in Figure 10-10.

Even if there is no transition or title, you can use the Precision Editor to fine-tune a cut point between two clips. Double-click in the space between the clips and the Precision Editor appears. This is the easiest way we know to trim the exact frames you want from one of your project's clips.

Figure 10-8:
A default
Fade to
White tran-
sition in the
Precision
Editor.

Figure 10-9:
The transi-
tion after
a pair of
adjust-
ments.

Figure 10-10:
The
Precision
Editor's
Extras
button lets
you see
what you've
added to
your proj-
ect's clips.

Adjusting audio separately from video

At times, you might want the audio from a clip to continue into the next clip. This might be for artistic effect or to block out a distracting noise at the start of a clip.

Industry folk often call such cuts *overlap edits* or *pre-lap* and *post-lap* edits (depending upon whether the sound starts prematurely or begins after the video). Other terms you might encounter are *J-cuts* and *L-cuts*, respectively. Now you know some more jargon to make you sound like an editing pro.

To adjust the audio of your clip separately from the video, proceed as follows:

1. **Open the Precision Editor by double-clicking the space between the two clips.**

   The Precision Editor pane appears.

2. **Click the Precision Editor's Audio button (see the margin).**

   Blue waveforms appear above the top filmstrip, as shown in Figure 10-11. These waveforms represent the audio tracks.

3. **Drag the line at the top waveform's cut point to the left to terminate its audio prematurely, or drag the line at the bottom waveform's cut point to the left to have it begin during the first clip, or to the right to have it begin after its associated video.**

   In Figure 10-12, we had the second clip's audio begin during the end of the first clip.

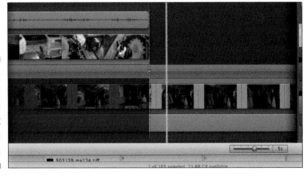

Figure 10-11: Blue waveforms represent the audio tracks.

Figure 10-12: Adjust the audio's cut points.

4. Click Done when you're finished to close the Precision Editor.

You can adjust both waveforms at the same time by pressing Shift while dragging an endpoint.

Using Picture-in-Picture

Jaded videophiles that we all are, we're accustomed to seeing *picture-in-picture* video, which is a small video frame superimposed on the full-screen. We see it on newscasts, where the anchorperson or correspondent is in the small frame telling us what's going on in the news footage that's playing. We also see it in documentaries, where the narrator describes what's being shown.

iMovie makes it simple to produce your own picture-in-picture footage. Here's how:

   1. **Make sure that Advanced Tools is selected in iMovie's General Preferences. Choose iMovie⇨Preferences (⌘+,) and click the General icon to check whether it's selected; select Show Advanced Tools if it isn't already selected.**

   You might save a trip to iMovie Preferences by looking at the iMovie toolbar to see whether the Arrow and Keyword tools are present — they're only on the toolbar when Advanced Tools are active.

   2. **Select the footage in the Events Browser that you want to have appear in the inset window.**

   3. **Drag the selected footage onto a clip in your project, as shown in Figure 10-13. A menu appears.**

Figure 10-13: Drag your inset footage over the clip where you want it to appear.

4. **Choose Picture in Picture, as shown in Figure 10-14.**

5. **The picture-in-picture clip sports a blue frame when it's not selected and appears above the footage it overlays, as shown in Figure 10-15. You can preview the PiP effect in the Viewer, as shown in Figure 10-16.**

Figure 10-14:
iMovie pres-
ents you
with some
options,
including
Picture in
Picture.

Figure 10-15:
A blue bor-
der signifies
a PiP clip.

Figure 10-16:
Et viola: You
have picture
in picture,
just like the
pros.

Now that you have your picture in picture in place, you can customize it in many ways:

- ✐ You can drag it in the project browser to start at another frame.
- ✐ You can drag the inset in the Viewer to another position on screen, as shown in Figure 10-17.

➣ Grab a corner handle on the inset and drag to resize the inset, as shown in Figure 10-18.

➣ Double-click the PiP clip in the project browser to customize how the inset appears and disappears from the screen as well as whether it has a border and how that border looks. Figure 10-19 shows the Clip Inspector with the PiP section (and the available PiP Effects).

Figure 10-17: Put the PiP inset where you want it on the screen by dragging.

Figure 10-18: Inset too large or too small? No problem, just drag a corner to resize it.

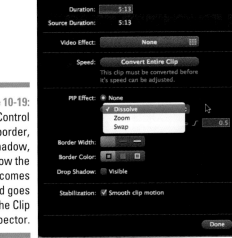

Figure 10-19: Control the border, shadow, and how the inset comes and goes in the Clip Inspector.

Swap is one of the coolest effects, providing a transition where the PiP clip takes over the screen, with the original footage shrinking into the inset and re-emerging at the end of the PiP clip.

Both clips' audio play simultaneously. Adjust the audio of either or both clips to control which audio is dominant. In a narration, for example, you would make the PiP clip's audio louder and duck the main clip's audio. Ducking is covered in Chapter 6.

If a PiP extends over a transition in your movie, the transition doesn't play.

Greening your screen

When you watch the weatherperson on TV, standing in front of the animated weather map, most of the time that map is actually just a solid green or blue background. When the weather forecast is broadcast, the weather maps replace the solid-colored section. The technical term for this effect, where a single color is made transparent so that other video can show through, is *chroma key*. You may also hear it called *greenscreen* or *bluescreen compositing*. Green and blue are the colors most frequently used because they provide such a small component of flesh tones. (This technique might not work so well if you're filming someone like a blue-skinned Orion alien for a *Star Trek* movie, though.)

To employ the greenscreen effect in your movies, proceed as follows:

1. **Record the video you want to superimpose against a green backdrop.**

   A highly saturated shade of green is best. You should make sure that the subject has no green in their attire, as the compositing process will also make those green areas become transparent. (St. Patrick's Day is not the best time to film your subject against the green backdrop.)

2. **Make sure iMovie's Advanced Tools are active (that is, that the Arrow tool is in the iMovie toolbar).**

   If they aren't, choose iMovie⇨Preferences, click General, and select Show Advanced Tools.

3. **Select the green background scene footage in the Event Browser.**

4. **Drag the selected footage to the clip in your project where you want it to appear. Choose Green Screen in the menu that appears (refer to Figure 10-14).**

   The greenscreen clip appears in your project above the video clip on which it will be superimposed and, when not selected, sports a dark green border, as shown in Figure 10-20.

A brief history of bluescreen compositing

Originally called *travelling matte*, the technique was such a breakthrough that its inventor, Larry Butler, received the Special Effects Oscar for it at the 1940 Academy Awards. And that wasn't the only Oscar awarded for the matte effect — in 1964, Petro Vlahos was awarded an Oscar for bluescreen compositing and then, at the end of the 1970s received an Emmy and a Lifetime Achievement Oscar for his work in compositing technology. Compositing allowed filmmakers to film, say, a whitewater rapids and place an actor's image into those rapids, or (like in *Raiders of the Lost Ark*) film a nest of vipers and superimpose Harrison Ford's green-screened scene on to it. Suffice it to say, digital compositing made many movie scenes possible that were too dangerous, too expensive, or too difficult to achieve "live."

---

5. **(Optional.) Select the greenscreen clip in your project and click the Cropped button that appears in the Viewer. Handles appear around your subject as shown in Figure 10-21. Drag the handles to surround your subject, making sure that he doesn't move out of that area elsewhere in the clip.**

6. **Click Done to exit the greenscreen editing process.**

If the last frame of your greenscreen clip contains only the bright green background and no subject, iMovie can use that information to improve the effect's efficacy. Double-click the greenscreen clip to invoke the Inspector, as shown in Figure 10-22. Select the Subtract Last Frame check box in the Background section. iMovie uses that information to further determine what gets subtracted from the greenscreen clip.

As with PiP clips, transitions that coincide with the greenscreen clip do not play.

Figure 10-20:
Green-
screen
clips have a
dark green
border and
sit above
the clip
they super-
impose.

Figure 10-21:
Adjust the
clipping box
around your
subject in
the Viewer.

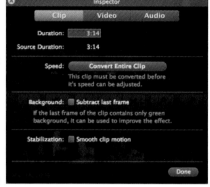

Figure 10-22:
The Clip
Inspector
with a
green-
screen clip
selected.

Cutting away

Yet another common video editing technique is the use of a *cutaway*, where you overlay video from one clip onto another. Basically, this boils down to replacing only the video (not the audio) from your primary footage with the alternate video. One common use is to replace some video of a performance with that of the audience to show reaction to what's occurring onstage.

Once again, iMovie makes implementing cutaways a piece of cake. Proceed as follows:

1. **Make sure that you have Advanced Tools active by checking to see if the Arrow and Keyword tools are present in the toolbar.**

    If they're not, choose iMovie⇨Preferences, display the General pane, and select the Show Advanced Tools checkbox.

2. **Select the cutaway footage in the Event Browser.**

3. **Drag the selected footage onto a clip in your project. From the menu shown in Figure 10-14, choose Cutaway.**

The cutaway clip, when not selected, sports a gray border and appears over the frames it will replace in your project. You can drag to reposition it, or you can drag the ends to lengthen or shorten the cutaway's duration.

4. **(Optional.) Double-click the cutaway clip to display the Clip Inspector, shown in Figure 10-23.**

You can adjust the fade in and fade out times by selecting the Manual radio button and then either typing a new duration in the associated text box or dragging the slider. You can also adjust the cutaway's translucency by dragging the Opacity slider — this can, if used judiciously, present a nice ghosted-image effect.

5. **Click Done when you're finished making your adjustments.**

iMovie gives you the cutaway shot's audio by default so, if you wish to maintain the audio from the original scene, you need to use the Audio Inspector to control which audio track is used.

Once again, if a transition coincides with a cutaway, the transition does not play.

Figure 10-23: The Clip Inspector when a cutaway clip is selected.

Replacing audio

Back in Chapters 1 and 2, when we recommended using multiple cameras, we were leading up to this brief discussion about audio. When you capture your footage from multiple sources, you give yourself options. You can choose which footage to use, but you can also opt to use the video from one with audio from another, or even just part of the audio from an alternate clip.

To replace a piece of flawed audio, select the frames with the bad audio in your project to determine how much audio you need to bring in from the other clip. This point is a good place to add a comment marker in your project. Then, proceed as follows:

1. **Make sure that you have Advanced Tools active by checking to see if the Arrow and Keyword tools are present in the toolbar.**

   If they are not active, choose iMovie⇨Preferences, display the General pane, and select the Show Advanced Tools check box.

2. **Select the frames from the clip in your Event Browser that have the good audio.**

3. **Drag the clip to the comment marker. The menu shown in Figure 10-14 once again appears.**

4. **Choose Audio Only.**

You've now replaced the inferior audio in your superior video clip with improved audio.

Another good use for audio replacement is a narration track.

Editing Audio

*I*n the classic movie musical *Singing in the Rain*, Jean Hagen plays Lina Lamont, a glamorous silent film star who, at the advent of talking pictures, is at risk of losing her career because she has a voice as ugly as her face is beautiful. The lesson is that even fantastic video footage can come to naught if the audio can't keep pace.

In the early chapters of this book, we repeatedly stress the importance of capturing quality audio. This might mean recording audio from multiple sources or employing external microphones to capture the audio up close and personal, even when the camera isn't.

Regardless, however, of how much care you take to obtain the best audio possible, sometimes "stuff happens." This chapter covers what iMovie offers to help you work around some of that stuff, including adjusting volume, normalizing volume across a clip (or clips), and setting beat markers to synchronize clips (and stills) with points in an audio track.

©Photodisc/Getty Images

Adjusting the Audio Volume

iMovie doesn't provide some audio editing features that were available in the iMovieHD and earlier versions, but it does include some new capabilities that are more useful, in general. For example, you can't manually *ramp* (gradually alter) a clip's audio up and down through a clip, but you can normalize volume across the clips in your project, fade the audio in and out at the ends of the clip, and duck the audio in other clips (see Chapter 6 for a discussion of ducking audio). Fortunately, if you're adept with GarageBand, you can work around the ramping limitation by duplicating your audio track, bringing it into GarageBand and editing it there, and then moving the result back to iMovie and replacing the original audio with the edited track.

The just-described workaround, thankfully, is one of the few workarounds remaining after the transition from the iMovieHD codebase to the new iMovie codebase in iLife '08, which required all sorts of audio editing workarounds. You even had to use GarageBand to add chapter markers to your movie in iMovie'08, but Apple returned chapter markers to iMovie in this version.

Normalizing clip volume

One of the great features added to iMovie'09, in our opinion, is the ability to normalize volume across a clip when in a project. *Normalizing* is the process of setting a clip's volume to a consistent level. If you have clips where the volume level differs noticeably, those clips are good candidates for normalization. Because most home video is shot using the camera's microphone rather than prepositioned microphones, the volume fluctuates depending on distance from the camera and which way the subject is facing relative to the microphone. Proceed as follows:

1. **Select the clip whose volume you wish to set to (roughly) the same level.**

2. **Invoke the Audio Inspector, as seen in Figure 11-1.**

   The easiest methods of invoking the Audio Inspector are to press A or double-click the selected clip, but you can also choose Window⇨Audio Adjustment or hover your mouse pointer near the beginning of the selected clip and choose Audio Adjustments from the Action (gear) menu that appears.

3. **Click Normalize Clip Volume.**

Figure 11-1: The Inspector's Audio pane is your sound booth.

After a clip's volume is normalized, you can use the Audio Inspector's Volume slider to raise or lower the volume. Although normalization makes the volume consistent, that consistent level hovers around the dominant level in the original clip, and that might be higher or lower than you want.

If you decide that the normalization isn't an improvement you wish to keep, click the Audio Inspector's Remove Normalization button at any time to restore the original audio levels.

Detaching a clip's audio

Although it doesn't often arise in our experience, when you want to work with a clip's audio track separately from the video, being able to detach the audio track is invaluable. You might need to reposition the audio, trim it, or duck a part of it. Whatever separate adjustment you might want to make, detaching the audio track from the video is the necessary first step in the process. Fortunately, it's easy to do:

1. **Select the video clip whose audio you wish to detach.**

2. **Choose Edit⇨Detach Audio.**

   The audio track appears below the clip as a purple bar, which you can see in Figure 11-2.

Figure 11-2:
A purple
detached
audio track.

A detached audio track

The term "detach audio" is slightly misleading. What's really happening is that iMovie makes a copy of the clip's audio track and then sets the clip's volume to zero. In other words, iMovie mutes the clip's audio track, just as though you had chosen Edit⇨Mute Clip (Shift+⌘+M) or set the volume to zero in the Audio Inspector. A side effect of this detachment method is that you can now boost the audio volume past the 200 percent limit imposed by the volume slider, as follows:

1. **Detach a clip's audio, as previously described.**

2. **Select the audio clip and display the Audio Inspector by any of the tried and true methods you prefer.**

3. **Move the volume slider to the right, past the 100 percent mark.**

This puts the total volume now over 200 percent (over 100 percent in the clip and 100 percent in the detached track).

4. **Adjust the detached track's volume similarly.**

Because you can move both sliders to 200 percent, you can achieve a cumulative level of up to 400 percent.

The preceding technique lets you recover from many situations where you have barely audible audio, but increased ambient noise accompanies your volume increase. We think that the trade-off is generally beneficial — although great audio is best, audible audio beats inaudible audio every time.

Keeping a Beat

As Michael will tell you, Dennis can't keep a beat in real life. Fortunately, iMovie lets him keep a digital beat in his video projects. *Beat markers* are the cornerstone to synchronizing your video with audio milestones, such as a clap of thunder, a particular line in a background song, or key points in a narrative.

To add a beat marker to any audio in your project, proceed as follows:

1. **Select an audio clip.**

If you want to set beat markers to the audio portion of an existing video clip, you must first detach the audio as described previously in this chapter and then select the detached audio clip.

2. **From the Action menu that appears when you hover over the beginning of your clip, choose Clip Trimmer. The Clip Trimmer opens, as shown in Figure 11-3.**

You could also choose Window➪Clip Trimmer, but we prefer not to have to move the mouse any farther than necessary.

A beat marker

Figure 11-3: The Clip Trimmer, with its beat marker identified by a tooltip.

Scoring with GarageBand

Film editors often use a temporary sound track for the score when editing a film, and then record the final score after the timing is set. You can use iMovie's ability to share a project with the Media Browser (see Chapter 12) to make your finished cut available in GarageBand, where you can then add the score, matching it precisely to your video.

When you choose to create a new project in GarageBand, one of your project type choices is a Movie project. A new Movie project comes with an empty movie. Drag your movie from the Media Browser in GarageBand to that empty track, and your movie appears as a series of thumbnails with its audio track visible below it.

You can then add music tracks to the movie, fading them in and out as needed. You can score your movie with the various music loops that GarageBand provides, play your own music, and even play sound effects from your keyboard.

This figure shows a simple movie project with two added music tracks: a jazz organ and strings. The volume levels of each track are set to fade in and out over one another, which is the audio equivalent of a visual dissolve.

When you finish scoring your movie, you can use GarageBand's Share menu to send the movie to iDVD, to iWeb, to iTunes, or to export it to disk. The last option gives you the ability to save the movie at full quality, so your final product looks just as good coming out of GarageBand as it did going in — and sounding even better!

Adding Audio from iTunes or GarageBand

iMovie and the Media Browser let you attach audio clips from your iTunes library and from GarageBand to your video. To display the audio that the Media Browser makes available, you can either choose Window⇨Music and Sound Effects (⌘+1) or just click the Music and Sound Effects toolbar button (the one with the musical note on it). Select the audio you want and drag it, as shown in the following figure, onto the clip where you want it to start playing. A green bar appears below the frames where the audio clip will play.

You can use the Media Browser's search field (at the bottom) to search for a sound effect or song by name or just scroll through the browser, previewing various audio pieces by clicking the Play button to the left of the search field.

3. **Drag a beat marker (the musical note in the Clip Trimmer's title bar, indicated in Figure 11-3) to the desired point in the waveform.**

   A thin vertical line with a dot in the center appears in your audio clip at the beat marker's position as well as in the Clip Trimmer waveform display.

   Although dragging the beat marker to your waveform is the true Mac way of achieving your goal, we would like to recommend the keyboard shortcut of just pressing M, which adds a beat marker at the playhead position in the Clip Trimmer.

4. **Repeat Step 3 for every beat marker you wish to set.**

5. **Reposition beat markers as desired by dragging them to new positions.**

6. **Preview as desired in the Clip Trimmer and click Done when you're satisfied.**

To remove a beat marker, display the Clip Trimmer and drag the beat marker off the waveform.

By default, iMovie has View➪Snap to Beats turned on (selected), as indicated by the check mark next to it in the View menu. This means that when you drag a clip or still into a project containing audio tracks with beat markers, the clip or still automatically aligns with the beat marker. One example of how to use this feature is to create title credits with background stills, with an optional Ken Burns Effect. Here's how:

1. **Add a song that you want to have as your title credits score.**

   See the sidebar, "Adding Audio from iTunes or GarageBand," to see how easy it is to use your existing music library to enhance your video project's audio.

2. **Set beat markers where you want your images and credits to appear.**

3. **Drag still images to the beat markers and apply titles to the stills as needed.**

   You can also add titles by themselves if you don't want an image behind it (for example, a traditional "over black" title screen). We cover adding stills in Chapter 7 and titles in Chapter 9.

Part IV
Production and Distribution

Digital Vision

In this part . . .

In these chapters, we focus on iDVD and cover the following topics:

✔ Chapter 12 details the ways you can share your movie on your Mac, on the Web, on portable devices, and on a DVD.

✔ Chapter 13 shows you two ways to make quick, no-fuss, no-muss DVDs from your video.

✔ Chapter 14 introduces iMovie's Themes and the theme-based approach to DVD authoring.

✔ Chapter 15 covers the actual DVD authoring process: adding and organizing your DVD's menus and arranging the buttons and text on those menus.

✔ Chapter 16 covers the last step in the process: burning your DVD so that you and others can enjoy it when it's inserted in a DVD player.

Sharing Your Movie

*W*hen we were kids, our parents and teachers taught us that sharing was a good thing, and we bet that yours did too. Current technology — the Internet, mobile devices, DVD players, and personal computers — provide a cornucopia of ways to share your videos, and Apple gave iMovie the tools to assist you in sharing your video wealth. And, as with most things Apple-related, sharing your movies is easy, as we describe in this chapter.

iTunes Is for Movies, Too

A few years ago, Apple expanded the iTunes mission statement, adding video to the plethora of audio types handled by planet Earth's best-known jukebox product. When your name and brand is as strong as the iTunes brand, you don't change its name just because you've expanded the product line; otherwise, Heinz would have stopped being Heinz when they added products other than pickles. So, don't let the name fool you. iTunes is not just for music — it's your movie library, too.

©iStockphoto|Константин Чагин

As your Mac's media nerve center, iTunes is an obvious place to enjoy and share your movies. Here's how to share your project with iTunes:

1. **Choose Share⇨iTunes.**

   iTunes displays the dialog shown in Figure 12-1.

Figure 12-1:
Use the
handy grid
to pick the
sizes you
want for
your movie.

2. **Select the sizes you want by clicking the appropriate check boxes, based upon how you're going to view your iTunes-hosted movie.**

   iTunes is your conduit to transfer your movie onto an iPod, an iPhone (or iPod Touch), or an AppleTV, in addition to being your Mac movie cataloger and viewing center. When you've selected a size, you can hover your mouse cursor over the circled *i* at the end of the row to see a tooltip detailing the codec used, the frame rate, the bit rate, and the estimated size, as shown in Figure 12-2.

   Squeezing data down in size is called *compression* and restoring it back to a usable form is called *decompression*. The software that performs compression and decompression is called a *codec* (compressor-decompressor). You can only compress data so much without losing part of it. A codec that gives you back exactly what you started with is referred to as *lossless*. A codec that discards data that is, hopefully, not discernible to the eye or ear when restored to a usable form is called *lossy*. JPEG image compression is probably the best known example of lossy compression.

   If you want to know more about codecs, not to mention frame rate and bit rate, check out the nearby sidebar, "Codecs and frame rates and bit-rates, oh my!"

3. **Click Publish.**

   iMovie displays the progress dialog shown in Figure 12-3.

   Don't be surprised if the initial time estimate seems fairly high — at first, iMovie doesn't have enough data sampled to make a very accurate estimate. The estimate comes down quite a bit after a bit of time elapses.

Figure 12-2:
The Info
button tells
you the
approximate
size of your
video and
other tech-
nical details.

Figure 12-3:
This prog-
ress dialog
tells you
which size
is being
exported
and (approx-
imately)
how much
longer the
process
will take.

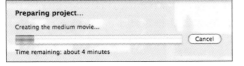

When iMovie is finished creating all the different specified sizes, the dialog rolls back up into the iMovie workspace's title bar and iTunes opens. Your movie is sitting in the iTunes Movies category, just waiting for you to watch it or send it on its way to one of your other devices, as shown in Figure 12-4.

You can now work in iTunes to distribute your movie to its various media centers, watch the movie, or just quit iTunes and go back to working in iMovie or some other application.

The type of dialog seen in Figures 12-1 and 12-3, where the dialog slides down out of the window's title bar and then slides back up when dismissed is what programmers, technical types, and assorted other nerds call a *sheet*. Now, if you hear someone being a little pretentious and telling you to click in the sheet, you can smile knowingly, click in the dialog, and rob them of the satisfaction of showing off their expertise by explaining yet another geeky term. You've seen lots of dialogs in this book, but we figured it was time to clue you in that some of them go by another name in techie circles.

Figure 12-4:
Here
you are,
with your
movie in
the iTunes
Movies
category.

If you look in your Project Library, you see an indicator that your project has been published and at what size, as shown in Figure 12-5, where you see the little square indicators just to the left of the thumbstrip showing that we published the Medium size (the second largest square).

Figure 12-5:
iMovie
indicates a
project has
been shared
and at what
size or sizes.

Indicates that your movie has been published and at what size.

If you no longer want your movie published to iTunes, select the project in iMovie and choose Share⇨Remove from iTunes. A spinning cursor appears: When it stops spinning, the movie is no longer in your iTunes library.

Codecs and frame rates and bit-rates, oh my!

For video and audio, MPEG (Motion Pictures Expert Group) compression is undoubtedly the pre-eminent format. But the video picture (pun intended) is more complicated than the still image arena. Three common MPEG formats exist (and a few that are far less common), with the not-so-original names MPEG-1, MPEG-2, and MPEG-4. (Don't ask about MPEG-3, it just never came to be.) If you've ever seen a VideoCD, you've encountered MPEG-1, and even if you haven't seen a VideoCD, you have benefited from the work that went into it. The ubiquitous MP3 audio file format stands for MPEG-1 audio layer 3 and took the audio world by storm in the 1990s and early 2000s, much to the initial consternation of the recording industry. DVD Video is almost always MPEG-2 (it can also be MPEG-1, but you seldom encounter commercial examples due to its lower quality). High definition television in the United States and a number of other countries is also MPEG-2, but there are some countries where MPEG-4 is broadcast due to its smaller size for the same quality (for example, Great Britain). Both MPEG-2 and MPEG-4 can be used on BluRay discs. The codec used for the MPEG-4 content that Apple supports on the iPod, iPhone, and AppleTV, as well as in iTunes is called H.264. For the trivia-inclined, this is sometimes called *MPEG-4 Part 10* or *MPEG-4 AVC* (for Advanced Video Codec). Another common MPEG-4 codec, supported on many DVD players and popular in the online world, is called *DivX* (it also has

a freeware equivalent called *xvid*). DivX is an example of MPEG-4 Part 2, also known as the Advanced Simple Profile (*ASP*). MPEG-4 Part 3 is the audio form that iTunes has as its default encoding format, more commonly known as *AAC* for Advanced Audio Codec. You can find out lots more about these terms online, but we're going to end our codec discussion here before our publisher tells us that this discussion has felled too many trees already.

As the *rate* parts of the terms *bit rate* and *frame rate* should indicate, these terms refer to time rather than space. We mentioned way back in Chapter 1 that frame rate tells how many still images pass the eye per second to give the illusion of continuous motion. If a frame rate is higher than about 16 fps (frames per second), the human eye and mind perceives continuity. Bit rate describes how much data, measured in bits (0s and 1s), is transferred per second. Common bit-rate examples are CD quality audio, which is 44.1 Kbps (44,100 bits per second), DVD Audio at 48 Kbps, and Blu-ray High-Def video and audio at between 48 Mbps and 54 Mbps (48,000,000 bps and 54,000,000 bps). That's a lot of 0s and 1s to transfer and process, and that's where the codecs we described previously come into play. The fewer bits your hardware has to read from the disc per second, the more it can process in memory and send to your screen. Remember: Memory is a *lot* faster than disc, hundreds to thousands of times faster.

Making Your Media Browsable in Other Applications

Just as iTunes is the nexus for sharing your content with devices such as the iPod or AppleTV, the aptly-named Media Browser is the means for sharing your media (sound, images, and video) with other applications, such as iDVD, iWeb, Keynote, and even non-Apple software products such as Roxio Toast Titanium. You've already seen the Media Browser in action in iMovie as the force behind the Music Browser and the Photo Browser (Chapter 8) and you'll see it again in this book's DVD coverage, coming soon in a chapter near you (er, that would be Chapter 13).

What became today's Media Browser began as a mechanism to share data between separate applications — iTunes, iPhoto, iMovie, and iDVD — when Apple bundled them together to create the iLife'04 product. Apple quickly realized that the browser could allow them to leverage iLife content elsewhere, such as in the Desktop and Accounts panes of System Preferences, the new Keynote presentation software, and even the professional media applications that now comprise the Final Cut Studio suite. Because programmers had to build the programming interfaces for it anyway, the rest of Apple's developer community also got access in the frameworks provided in Xcode, the Mac OS X development environment.

Apple is appropriately fond of using effective and consistent interface elements, so what you're about to see is likely to be very familiar. To share your project to the Media Browser, proceed as follows:

1. **Choose Share⇨Media Browser.**

   The dialog shown in Figure 12-6 slides down out of your workspace's title bar.

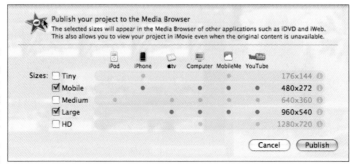

Figure 12-6: The Publish Your Project to the Media Browser dialog.

2. **Select the size or sizes you want to publish by checking the appropriate check boxes.**

   You might note that there are a couple of extra columns in the grid compared to Figure 12-1. That's because iTunes handles hardware and the Media Browser handles all the formats needed for iTunes as well as formats used by applications other than iTunes, such as iWeb. Additionally, in the iMovie 8.0.1 update, Apple added a high-definition (HD) export option for sharing via the Media Browser. The HD choice is not available when sharing with iTunes, iDVD, YouTube, or the MobileMe Gallery, but comes in really handy if you have a way to author high-definition video, such as Toast Titanium's optional Blu-ray plug-in.

Look back to Figure 12-2 to see what hovering your mouse pointer over the info button at the end of a row displays about the video you're sharing.

3. **Click Publish to start publishing your project for use by the Media Browser.**

   The progress dialog shown back in Figure 12-3 as well as the accompanying discussion also applies here.

The Project Library pane, shown in Figure 12-7, displays that our project has been published in the three largest sizes: Mobile, Medium, and Large.

Figure 12-7:
The Project
Library
tracks all
the sizes
in which a
project is
published.

This video has been published in Mobile, Medium, and Large.

If you no longer want your movie, or a particular size or set of sizes, to be available via the Media Browser, select the project in iMovie and choose Share➪Remove from Media Browser. The Remove Rendered Movies from the Media Browser dialog appears. Select the sizes that you no longer want published and click Remove.

Channeling YouTube

Few Web sites achieve superstar status: Amazon (www.amazon.com) is king of Internet retailing, Yahoo! (www.yahoo.com) and Google (www.google.com) dominate search, MySpace (www.myspace.com) and Facebook (www.facebook.com) reign in the social networking realm, and eBay (www.ebay.com) dominates the auction scene. But the Big Kahuna of Web video sharing has to be YouTube (www.youtube.com).

If you already have a YouTube account (called a *channel*, in keeping with the TV metaphor), publishing your iMovie video is a piece of cake. If you don't have a channel, you need to register to get one before you can upload your movie to YouTube. Creating a YouTube account is discussed in the sidebar elsewhere in this chapter, "Creating a YouTube Account." After you have that account, proceed as follows to share your video:

1. Choose Share⇨YouTube.

The Publish Your Project to YouTube dialog drops down out of the iMovie title bar, as shown in Figure 12-8.

If your movie is longer than 10 minutes, a notice warning that your movie may be rejected by YouTube displays in the lower-left corner of the dialog, as seen in Figure 12-8. Click Cancel and shorten the movie in iMovie before trying to publish to YouTube or you'll encounter the dialog shown in Figure 12-9 after Step 10 and you'll have to start over, anyway.

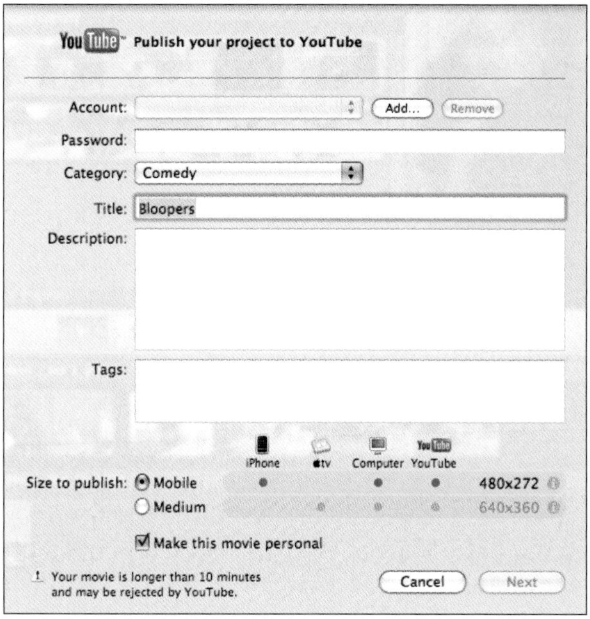

You Tube™ **Publish your project to YouTube**

Account: ⬍ (Add...) (Remove)
Password:
Category: Comedy ⬍
Title: Bloopers
Description:

Tags:

iPhone ▪tv Computer YouTube
Size to publish: ● Mobile   ●   ●   ●   480x272 ⓘ
                 ○ Medium   ⬤   ⬤   ⬤   640x360 ⓘ
☑ Make this movie personal
! Your movie is longer than 10 minutes   (Cancel) (Next)
  and may be rejected by YouTube.

Figure 12-8: The YouTube publishing dialog.

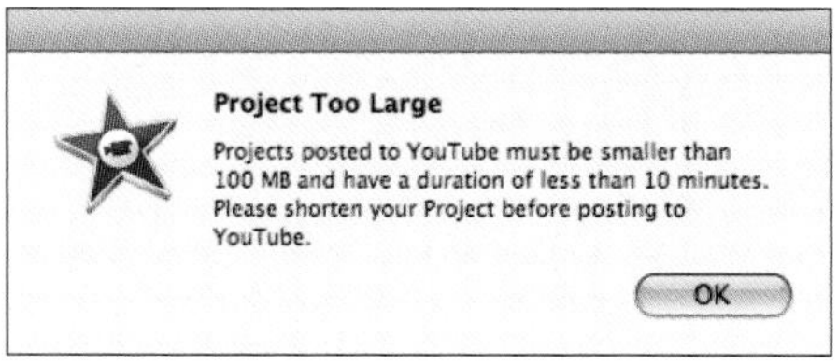

Figure 12-9: Go back and start over: Your movie exceeded YouTube's size or length limit.

Project Too Large
Projects posted to YouTube must be smaller than 100 MB and have a duration of less than 10 minutes. Please shorten your Project before posting to YouTube.

(OK)

2. If you have a YouTube or Google account (Google purchased YouTube in 2006) that iMovie already knows about, skip to Step 4. If not, click the Add button next to the Account drop-down list box to specify one.

The Add Account pane appears as shown in Figure 12-10. If you don't have a YouTube account, go to `www.youtube.com` and create one as described in the nearby sidebar, "Creating a YouTube Account."

YouTube Publish your project to YouTube
Add Account
Enter a YouTube user account name
Cancel
Done

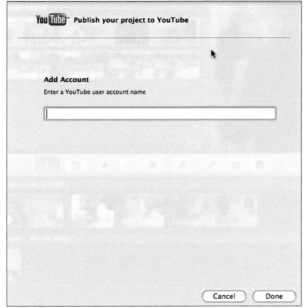

Figure 12-10: Enter a YouTube user account name.

3. **Enter an account name in the text box and click Done.**
4. **In the Publish Your Project to YouTube dialog, choose a category from the Category pop-up shown in Figure 12-11.**

✓ Comedy
Travel & Events
Autos & Vehicles
People & Blogs
Sports
Pets & Animals
Entertainment
Science & Technology
News & Politics
Howto & Style
Nonprofits & Activism
Education
Gaming
Music
Film & Animation

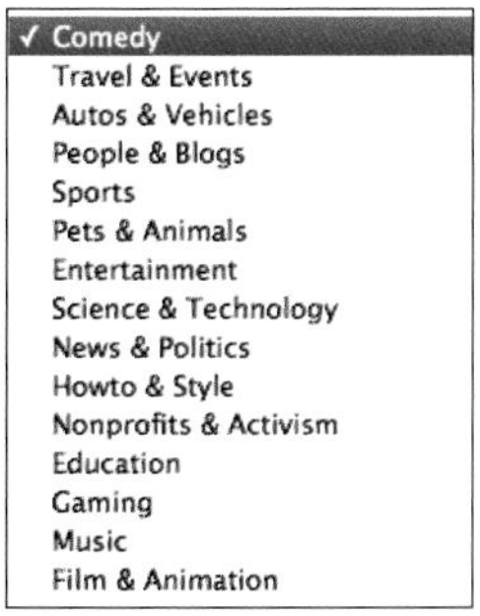

Figure 12-11: The YouTube movie categories.

5. **Fill in the Title text field.**

   iMovie places your project's name in the field by default — you can, of course, accept the suggestion or supply your own.

6. **(Optional, but recommended.) Fill in the Description and Tags text boxes.**

   Tags are keywords that YouTube viewers can search on to find your video.

7. **Select either Mobile or Medium as your movie's size.**

8. **If you want to restrict your movie's viewers to those specified by your YouTube account, leave the Make This Movie Personal check box selected. To allow any YouTube visitor to view your movie, deselect the check box.**

9. **Click Next. The YouTube Terms of Service agreement appears.**

10. **If you wish to continue, click Publish.**

    Assuming all is well, you'll see a progress dialog marking the encoding and uploading process. When processing is complete, iMovie presents the dialog shown in Figure 12-12.

Figure 12-12:
Success!
Your movie
is now on
YouTube.

Your video has been uploaded to YouTube. It may be several minutes or hours before your video is processed and viewable, depending on YouTube's server load.

Your video can be viewed at: http://www.youtube.com/watch?v=r0F-Jp8X7fY

Tell a Friend | View | OK

11. **Click OK to dismiss the dialog and get back to work, click View to have your Web browser take you to your movie on YouTube, or click Tell a Friend to invoke your e-mail client and send a notification missive out to your adoring fans.**

If (or when) you no longer want your video on YouTube, select your project in iMovie and choose Share➪Remove from YouTube. iMovie displays a dialog telling you that you have to remove your video from your My Videos page on YouTube before clicking Done. Click the Go to YouTube button and your Web browser opens to www.youtube.com. Sign into YouTube, if you're not already, and you are taken to your My Videos page. Select the check box next to the movie you want to remove and click the Delete link. Confirm the deletion in the dialog that appears and return to the iMovie workspace to click the Done button.

Creating a YouTube account

You need either a registered YouTube or Google account (Google owns YouTube, after paying a mere $1.65 billion) to post your videos to YouTube. If you don't have either, you can create a YouTube account by visiting www. youtube.com and clicking the Sign In link that appears near the top right of the page. A secure page on www.google.com appears bearing a Sign Up for YouTube link near the bottom right of the page. Click that link to bring up the Create Your YouTube Account page. Fill in the blanks. You need to select the check box indicating that you accept YouTube's Terms of Use and Privacy Policy (the Privacy Policy is pretty much the expected boiler-plate, but you should at least check out the Terms of Service to know what kinds of videos are and are not allowed). Click the Create Account button. You receive an e-mail from YouTube to verify the account. Click the link in the e-mail message to verify it and your browser takes you back to www.youtube.com. You now have an account.

By the way, Apple's iMovie Help tells you that clicking Add in the YouTube publishing dialog takes you to YouTube's Web site to create the account, but it doesn't. You need to make the visit on your own, thus this sidebar.

Using MobileMe to Share

 If you have one of Apple's MobileMe accounts, you can publish your movies directly to your MobileMe Gallery. MobileMe enables you to enjoy all the bells and whistles of iLife in addition to the more mundane e-mail, iDisk, syncing, and so forth features, and we think it's a great investment (especially if you subscribe at the discounts available through Amazon and other online retailers). If you don't have a MobileMe account yet, you can (at least at the time we're writing this) get a 60-day trial by visiting www.apple.com/mobileme and clicking on the Free Trial link. MobileMe is priced at $99/year, but the Amazon price is $63.50 at present (as of April 2009). As of this writing, it's at the top-right corner of the page, but Web pages change frequently, so if you don't find it there, look around a bit.

Publishing your movie to your MobileMe Gallery is, as usual, straightforward, but there are a few steps to the process:

1. **Choose Share⊏➪MobileMe Gallery.**

   If you are signed into your MobileMe account, you see the dialog shown in Figure 12-13. Otherwise, you see the dialog in Figure 12-14, giving you a chance to sign in, if you have a subscription, or to get a free trial by clicking the Learn More button and signing up.

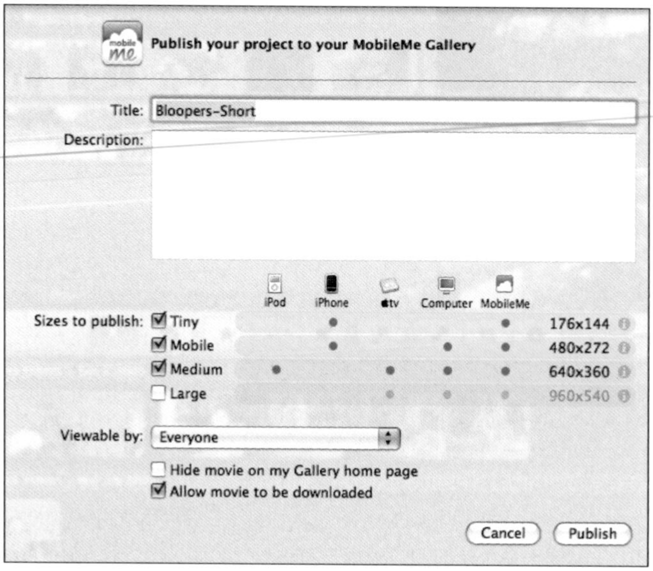

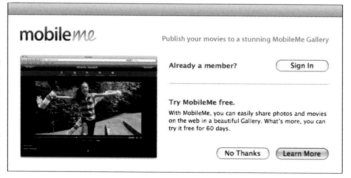

Figure 12-13:
Establish
your
MobileMe
publishing
parameters
here.

Figure 12-14:
Not signed
in to
MobileMe
or in need of
an account?

2. **Either accept the project name as the title or enter a new one in the Title text box.**

3. **(Optional.) Tell people about your movie in the Description text box.**

4. **Pick one or more sizes to publish.**

   Check boxes for already-encoded sizes are preselected, letting you know that they don't require re-encoding.

5. **Choose who can view your movie in the Viewable By pop-up menu.**

   You can choose Everyone, Only Me, or Edit Names and Passwords. If you choose the latter, you see the Names and Passwords dialog in Figure 12-15. The Names and Passwords dialog gives clear and straightforward instructions, so we won't belabor them here.

Figure 12-15:
Assign
names and
passwords
to restrict
access to
your movie.

6. **Back in the Publish Your Project to Your MobileMe Gallery dialog, if you don't want the movie to appear on your Gallery's home page, select the Hide Movie on My Gallery Home Page check box.**

7. **If you want visitors to your movie's Web page to be able to download a copy of the movie, leave the Allow Movie to Be Downloaded check box selected; otherwise, deselect it.**

8. **Click Publish.**

   iMovie encodes and uploads your movie to your MobileMe Gallery, displaying the usual progress dialogs. After the movies are finished uploading to MobileMe, iMovie displays the dialog shown in Figure 12-16. Clicking the Tell a Friend button invokes your e-mail program so that you can send out an *e-nnouncement* (our made-up term for this ubiquitous feature). View takes you to your movie using your Web browser, and OK just dismisses the dialog so that you can get back to work or play.

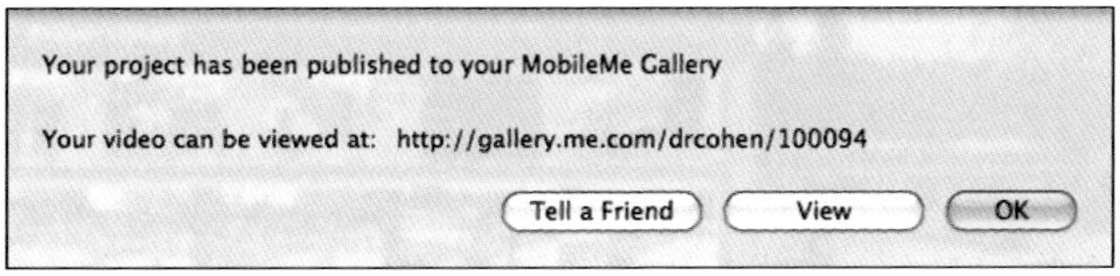

Figure 12-16:
Tell friends,
check it out
yourself, or
just get
on with
your day.

Your project has been published to your MobileMe Gallery

Your video can be viewed at: http://gallery.me.com/drcohen/100094

(Tell a Friend)   (View   )   (OK   )

If you no longer want the movie on MobileMe, select your project in iMovie and choose Share➪Remove from MobileMe Gallery. iMovie displays a confirmation dialog telling you that the operation cannot be undone. Click Continue to perform the removal or Cancel to leave it published.

Sharing Movies Old-School with iDVD

Sharing video on the Web, either via MobileMe or YouTube, is great, assuming that all the people with whom you want to share have good Internet access (broadband is highly recommended for video) and, in the case of MobileMe, are running relatively current Web browsers. (Further, to make your video permanently available, you have to keep the account going in perpetuity and have the space your movie occupies unavailable for new movies or other use.) However, if you want Grandma and Grandpa to see the video and have it as a permanent keepsake, it's probably time to get physical, and that means sending them a DVD that they can watch on their TV set (or computer).

Sharing via iDVD is very simple. Just proceed as follows:

1. **Choose Share➪iDVD.**

   iMovie presents the progress dialog shown in Figure 12-17, telling you that it is preparing the movie for iDVD.

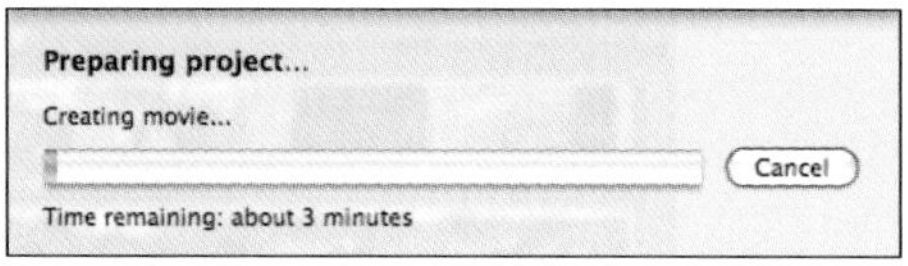

Figure 12-17:
iMovie lets
you know
that it's
preparing
your project
for use with
iDVD.

> Preparing project...
>
> Creating movie...
>
> [ ] (Cancel)
>
> Time remaining: about 3 minutes

2. **When complete, iDVD launches and your movie is automatically placed in an iDVD project, as shown in Figure 12-18.**

   This is where placing chapter markers, as described in Chapter 10, pays big dividends. As we explain in Chapters 13 and 14, iDVD automatically creates submenus so that your DVD's audience can navigate directly to scenes of interest.

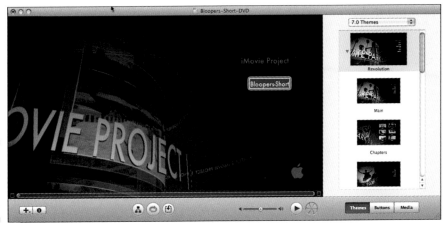

Figure 12-18:
Your movie
is now in
iDVD.

This seems like an excellent place to end this chapter — the next Part of this book tells you how to use iDVD to create DVDs of your movies.

13

Making a Quick DVD

*I*t seems as though DVD technology has been around for eons, but, as we write this book, it's really only about fifteen years old! Time sure flies when you're having fun.

Nonetheless, many people feel DVDs are passé, if not completely moribund, especially in the face of HDTV, Blu-ray discs, and streaming video services such as YouTube (www.youtube.com) and Hulu (www.hulu.com). In fact, Apple itself seems ambivalent about the DVD format: iDVD is the only one of all the components of iLife '09 that didn't get even a minor update from the previous version of iLife.

But, unlike Monty Python's famous parrot, DVD is not resting, nor is it pining for the fjords. It is a stable, mature technology, and still one of the best ways to get your video creations into the hands of your friends and family.

That leaves the question, "How do you *get* the video onto a DVD in the first place?" In the previous chapter, we cover one way: via the Share menu in iMovie. In this chapter, you're going to get a look at two other options.

©iStockphoto/Amanda Rhode

Using Magic iDVD

Like other applications in the iLife suite, iDVD keeps track of what you were working on, and it opens that project when you start iDVD. But if you have no previous project for iDVD to open, or if you close your current project, you see the window shown in Figure 13-1.

This window contains the button with which this particular section of the book is concerned: the Magic iDVD button.

Click the Magic iDVD button, and iDVD presents the drag-and-drop Magic iDVD window as shown in Figure 13-2.

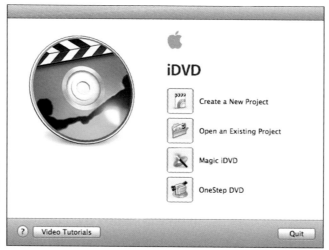

Figure 13-1:
Where you
begin with
iDVD.

Figure 13-2:
The Magic
iDVD
window.

On this simple screen, you can add the media — movies and photos — that you want to appear on your DVD. You can also specify the title of your DVD and choose the theme that controls the appearance of the DVD's menu screens and menu buttons.

On a DVD, a menu refers to a screen that contains buttons. You use your DVD player's remote control to select a button on a menu in order to see another menu, to play a movie, to view a scene in a movie, or to play a DVD slideshow (that is, a collection of photographs on the DVD that play with optional background music).

And where do you get the media to put on the DVD? One place is the iLife Media Browser, which appears on the right side of the Magic iDVD window, as shown in Figure 13-3.

Figure 13-3:
The iDVD
Media
Browser.

The Media Browser offers you the following media:

- **Audio:** These sources include your GarageBand compositions and any audio in your iTunes library.
- **Photos:** Sources for these are your iPhoto library and your Aperture library.
- **Movies:** The Media Browser displays your iMovie Projects and Events, video from your iPhoto Library, video from your iTunes Library, and any other video files in your home directory's Movies folder.

Not all video and audio files from these sources are available in the Media Browser, however. iMovie projects and GarageBand compositions need to be shared explicitly with the Media Browser in order for them to be available to iDVD. For example, you need to use iMovie's Share⇨Media Browser command and specify the output size of a movie before the iDVD Media Browser can offer it. Otherwise, you see the message shown in Figure 13-4 when you click the iMovie project in the Media Browser.

You are not limited to the Media Browser as a media source for iDVD. You can use video, audio, and photos from anywhere on your Mac. Just drag the media from a Finder window into your DVD project.

To build a DVD project with Magic iDVD, follow these steps:

1. **Drag one or more movies from the Media Browser to the Drop Movies Here strip in the left side of the Magic iDVD window.**

   You can shift-click or ⌘-click to select multiple movies to drag, as shown in Figure 13-5. The number of movies being dragged appears beside your pointer as you drag.

2. **Optionally, drag one or more selections of photos to the Drop Photos Here strip.**

   Each group of photos that you drop on the strip becomes a DVD slide-show, represented by a thumbnail, as shown in Figure 13-6. Note that if you drop photos on top of an existing slideshow in the strip, those photos are added to that slideshow. An iDVD slideshow can have as many as 9,801 slides.

   In fact, a DVD can contain no more than 9,801 images. If, for some odd reason, you put that many images in a single slideshow, you won't be able to create any more slideshows in your iDVD project.

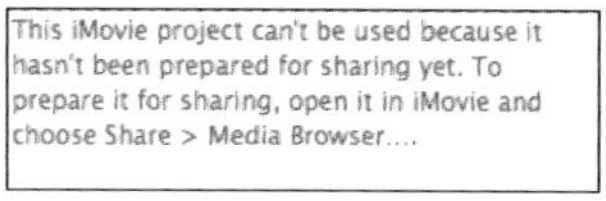

Figure 13-4:
This movie's not for sharing.

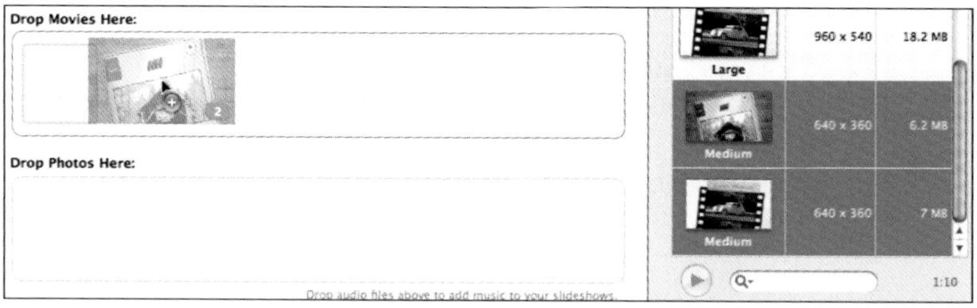

This iMovie project can't be used because it hasn't been prepared for sharing yet. To prepare it for sharing, open it in iMovie and choose Share > Media Browser....

Figure 13-5:
Drag and drop movies to add them to your DVD.

Drop Movies Here:

Drop Photos Here:

Drop audio files above to add music to your slideshows

960 x 540   18.2 MB
Large

640 x 360   6.2 MB
Medium

640 x 360   7 MB
Medium

1:10

You can also drag and drop audio from the Media Browser onto a slideshow thumbnail in the Drop Photos Here strip. The audio becomes the background audio for that slideshow presentation. An audio icon appears on the slideshow thumbnail when you drop audio on it.

3. **In the DVD Title box at the top of the screen, type a name for your DVD.**

4. **Select a theme for your DVD.**

   The available themes, by default, are those from the most recent version of iDVD. However, you can choose theme collections from other versions of iDVD from the menu to the right of the theme scroller, and even show all of the themes at once, as shown in Figure 13-7.

   When you install iDVD, you have the option of installing additional iDVD media. If you don't install that media, you only have the most recent iDVD themes available to you.

5. **In the lower-right of the Magic iDVD window, click Create Project.**

   After you click the Create Project button, iDVD prepares the project for you. When it is finished, the Magic iDVD window is replaced by the project window for your iDVD project. Figure 13-8 shows a project window created by Magic iDVD.

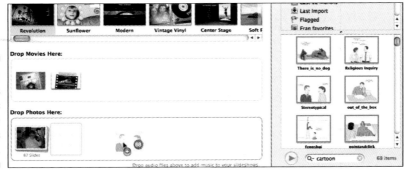

Figure 13-6:
Drop groups
of photos
to create
slideshows
on the DVD.

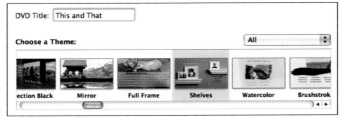

Figure 13-7:
Give your
project a
title and a
theme.

Figure 13-8:
A project
created by
Magic iDVD.

At this point, you can customize the project or just burn the DVD; see Chapter 14 and Chapter 15 to find out how to customize a project and see Chapter 16 to discover how to burn a DVD project.

Creating a OneStep DVD

For even more instant gratification, you can use iDVD's OneStep DVD feature — if, that is, you have both of the following items:

- ✔ **A video camera with a FireWire connector:** Many recent video cameras have only USB connectors.

- ✔ **A Mac with a FireWire port:** Some recent MacBook models do not have FireWire ports.

- ✔ **The proper cables and adapters:** There are at least three different types of FireWire connectors — the four-pin FireWire 400 connector (sometimes called iLink), the six-pin FireWire 400 connector, and the new(ish) nine-pin FireWire 800 connector. Adapters exist to convert from any of these to any other, but you have to have the right ones for your camera and computer.

Assuming that you do have what you need, you can make a DVD in only a few steps — not quite the one step that the feature name would have you believe, but in very few steps. This feature creates a DVD from all of the footage in your camera without putting you to the bother of setting up an iDVD project at all.

The OneStep DVD button appears on the iDVD start screen, shown at the beginning of this chapter in Figure 13-1. Figure 13-9 shows you the message you get when you click the OneStep DVD button without having a camera connected.

Figure 13-9:
iDVD tells
you how
to use
OneStep
DVD.

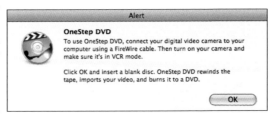

Alert

OneStep DVD
To use OneStep DVD, connect your digital video camera to your computer using a FireWire cable. Then turn on your camera and make sure it's in VCR mode.

Click OK and insert a blank disc. OneStep DVD rewinds the tape, imports your video, and burns it to a DVD.

OK

The message says everything you need to know: Follow those instructions, wait for iDVD to recognize the disc, and then sit back as iDVD takes control of your camera.

By the way — we count six steps to this process (seven if you have to insert the tape into the camera):

1. **On the iDVD start screen, click OneStep DVD.**

2. **Connect your camera to your Mac.**

3. **Turn the camera on.**

4. **Put the camera into VCR mode.**

5. **Click OK.**

6. **Insert a blank disc into your Mac's DVD burner.**

iDVD rewinds the tape in the camera to the beginning, so don't expect to queue up a scene on the tape and just capture the video from there.

Figure 13-10 shows the dialog that appears as iDVD works its way through the recording. The dialog shows the amount of material captured so far and the amount of time available on the DVD. This second figure depends on the capacity of the recordable DVD and may be quite inaccurate at the beginning of the capture process.

Figure 13-10:
Capturing
the OneStep
DVD video.

Creating your OneStep DVD

⊖ Capture Movie
● Prepare DVD
● Process Movie
● Burn

00:00:00:20 captured, 13:36:48 available

Time remaining : ---

Stop

Although OneStep DVD always captures from the beginning of the tape, you don't have to capture the entire contents. You can press Stop at any time, which produces the dialog shown in Figure 13-11.

Figure 13-11:
Clicking
Stop lets
you burn
what you've
captured.

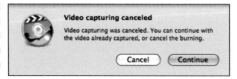

After capturing is complete, iDVD encodes the video that it has captured and burns it to the DVD. This process can take several hours, depending on the amount of video captured and the speed of your Mac. (You can, by the way, turn off your camera and disconnect it after iDVD has begun encoding the video that it has captured.)

Make sure that you have plenty of storage available on your Mac's startup drive. iDVD stores the captured video in a temporary location on that drive, and a full tape can consume many gigabytes of storage: as much as twenty-four gigabytes for ninety minutes of imported video along with the encoded copy that gets burned to the DVD.

When iDVD finishes burning the disc, it ejects it and gives you the opportunity of burning another copy. This copy uses the previously encoded video, so burning a second DVD doesn't take nearly as long.

And what do you get when you make such a DVD? You get a DVD with a generic name (see the icon in the left margin) that is set to play automatically when you insert it in a DVD player or open it with your Mac's DVD Player application.

14

Working with iDVD Themes

*i*DVD provides you with a number of carefully crafted, professionally designed themes that you use to create the look of your iDVD project. These themes provide designs for menu screens, buttons, and highlights.

Much like iMovie themes, iDVD themes give you a running start on designing your DVD. (We cover iMovie themes in Chapter 8.) But unlike iMovie themes, which you can use or not use as you like, you *have* to take that running start with iDVD: You can't make a DVD without choosing an Apple theme as your starting point.

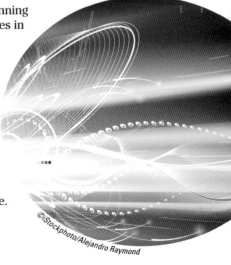

©iStockphoto/Alejandro Raymond

Don't worry — Apple isn't out to cramp your style completely. You can discard many of the elements that an iDVD theme provides and you can override others. Although you must start with an Apple theme, you can end up with a DVD design that is more or less your own. And you can even save your DVD design as a theme for future use.

Selecting a Theme

Apple gives you quite a few DVD themes from which to choose. You get ten themes from iDVD version 7.0 (the version of iDVD that comes with iLife '08 and iLife '09), ten more themes from iDVD version 6.0, and, if you want them, dozens of themes from iDVD versions even earlier than that.

When you create an iDVD project, you can see the available themes in the iDVD project window by clicking the Themes button at the lower right. This displays the theme thumbnails in the pane above the button, as shown in Figure 14-1.

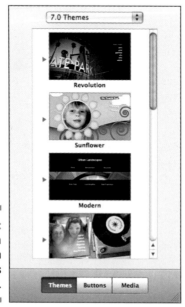

Figure 14-1:
Pick a
theme from
the Themes
Browser.

To select a theme for a new project, simply click the theme in the Themes pane. iDVD immediately applies the theme to your project.

Strictly speaking, the term *theme* applies to a single menu design. A collection of related themes are more accurately referred to as *theme families*, although iDVD often uses *theme* to refer either to a single menu design or to the theme family to which the menu design belongs.

Each iDVD theme family comprises menu designs that include the following:

- **Background graphics:** Each menu design has a background graphic over which the menu elements are displayed. As we explain in the section, "Customizing a Theme," later in this chapter, you can replace these with graphics of your own choosing.

- **Default fonts:** The menu buttons and titles that you place on a DVD menu use specific fonts in specific sizes and styles chosen to harmonize with the theme design. However, you can override these as well, as we cover in Chapter 15.

⌐ **Menu button designs:** By default, the menu button designs for each theme are text buttons that use the menu's default font. You can, however, apply different button designs, including designs that incorporate video loops. Chapter 15 explains how to do this.

The theme families installed with iDVD can also include the following:

⌐ **Video animation:** The default iDVD theme families incorporate *motion menus*, which play animations in a loop over the background graphic. The loops often contain an *intro* — an animation that plays when the menu first appears on screen — and an *outro* — an animation that plays when the menu leaves the screen. You can enable or disable these, and control the length of the animation loop, as explained later in "Customizing a Theme."

⌐ **Background audio:** The motion menu animations frequently are accompanied with an audio loop that plays while the menu is on the screen. You can eliminate the audio, adjust its volume, or replace the audio track with audio of your own choosing, as we explain later in the section entitled "Customizing a Theme."

⌐ **Drop zones:** Most menu designs have ornamental *drop zones* into which you can drop video or still images. These drop zones serve no functional purpose, providing only additional eye-catching menu animation. You edit drop zones with iDVD's drop zone editor, or you can suppress the display of a menu's drop zones, as described later in — you guess it — "Customizing a Theme."

Each theme family in the iDVD default installation comes with several related menu designs that you can use for specific purposes. Figure 14-2 shows the Shelves theme family from the iDVD 6.0 theme collection, expanded to show the three menu designs that belong to the family.

Figure 14-2:
A theme
family
expanded.

Shelves

Main

Chapters

Extras

The three menu designs in a typical iDVD theme family comprise the following:

- **Main:** You typically use the Main menu design for the main screen that your user sees, and the screen that the DVD returns to when the user clicks the Title button on the DVD player's remote control. The main menu contains menu buttons that link to the primary contents of the DVD, such as the featured movie or slideshow. Main menus frequently have menu buttons that lead to submenus containing additional DVD content.

- **Chapters:** You use a Chapters menu to offer the user menu buttons that lead to individual scenes in the DVD's featured movie. When you add a movie to your iDVD that has chapter markers, iDVD automatically creates one or more Chapters menus that contain menu buttons for the individual chapters in the movie.

- **Extras:** You use this kind of menu for additional DVD features, such as secondary movies or slideshows.

Menus that you access from the main DVD menu are often referred to as *submenus*.

You don't have to use every menu design in your project. Many DVD projects can get by with just a single Main menu. In fact, many of the older, optional themes that come with iDVD contain only a single menu design. These are useful for simple DVD projects.

And speaking of older, optional themes, here's how you can get them:

1. **From the menu at the top of the Themes pane, choose Old Themes.**

   The optional themes appear in the pane, dimmed, as shown in Figure 14-3.

Figure 14-3:
Older optional themes appear dim in the Themes pane if they aren't installed.

2. **Click any of the dimmed theme thumbnails.**

   A dialog appears that offers you theme installation options. You have the following options:

   - **Download Now:** Choose this to launch the Software Update application to download and install the themes.

   - **Download Later:** Choose this to have the themes appear in the Software Update application the next time you run it.

   - **Install from DVD:** Choose this to install the themes from your iLife '09 installation DVD.

3. **Click an option in the dialog and then click OK.**

The optional themes require 700MB of disk storage. Naturally, using either of the download options also requires an active Internet connection.

You may have some trouble with these older themes. Neither of us have gotten the download options in iDVD to work with some of the old themes: Software Update simply tells us that our software is up to date. What's more, if you received your copy of iDVD with a new Mac, you won't have a separate iLife installation DVD. Instead, you have to find the iDVD installation package on the Install or Restore DVD that came with your Mac.

Changing Themes

Picking a theme does not lock you in to your choice forevermore: You can change the theme of an individual menu or of the entire project at any time.

Figure 14-4 shows the main menu of the iDVD project that we created to demonstrate Magic iDVD in Chapter 13. The project uses the Shelves theme from the 6.0 Themes collection.

Figure 14-4: A main menu from a project using the Shelves theme.

This and That

Movies

Slideshows

Figure 14-5 shows the same project after we applied the Forever theme from the 7.0 Themes collection.

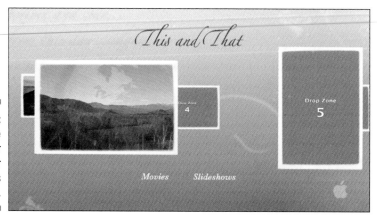

Figure 14-5:
The same menu after the Forever theme is applied.

As you can see, iDVD moved the title text and the menu buttons around to match the new theme's layout, and retained the contents of the three drop zones from the old theme but left the others empty, waiting for content.

To apply a different theme to an existing project, simply click the theme family you want to apply in the Themes pane. iDVD displays the dialog shown in Figure 14-6. Note the helpful advice you see when you expand the dialog: You can change the themes of all of a project's menus, or apply a theme to individual menus on a case-by-case basis.

Figure 14-6:
iDVD may ask to confirm a change of theme.

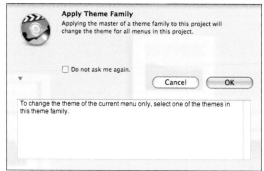

Apply Theme Family
Applying the master of a theme family to this project will change the theme for all menus in this project.

☐ Do not ask me again.

▼   (Cancel)   (OK)

To change the theme of the current menu only, select one of the themes in this theme family.

iDVD's General preferences offers a set of options that apply to theme changes:

1. **Choose iDVD⇨Preferences, or press ⌘+comma (,) and then click General.**

2. **Click one of the When Changing Themes options:**

   - **Use theme default values:** Select this to have iDVD use only the theme's design styles for all menu elements and ignore any customizations you may have made to the menu and the elements on it.

   - **Retain changes to theme defaults:** Select this option to have iDVD respect any customized elements. For example, if you change the size and font of a text title on the main menu, the title retains those settings when the theme changes.

   - **Always ask:** iDVD asks you what to do about changed menu elements when you switch themes.

3. **Close the Preferences window.**

When you switch to a theme designed for a different aspect ratio than the one your project uses, iDVD asks you if you want to switch to the new theme's native aspect ratio, as shown in Figure 14-7. Changing aspect ratios is discussed in the next section.

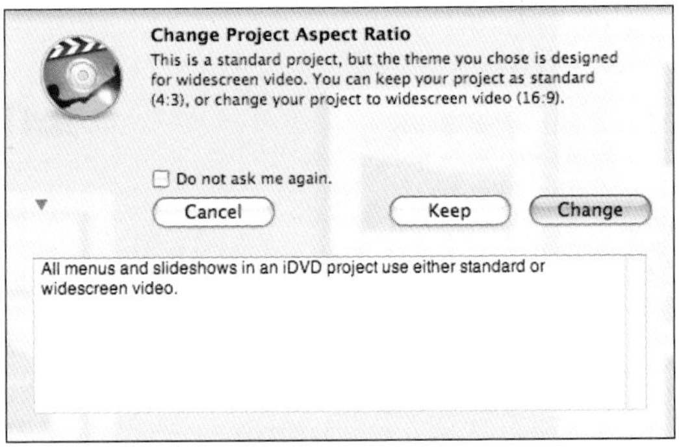

Change Project Aspect Ratio
This is a standard project, but the theme you chose is designed for widescreen video. You can keep your project as standard (4:3), or change your project to widescreen video (16:9).

☐ Do not ask me again.

[Cancel]   [Keep]   (Change)

All menus and slideshows in an iDVD project use either standard or widescreen video.

Figure 14-7:
Changing to a theme with a different aspect ratio.

Customizing a Theme

There are lots of ways to override the menu design imposed by the theme that you have chosen. The key to many of these changes is the Inspector window.

The Inspector window is a most useful tool in iDVD, and, as befitting its importance, you can invoke it multiple ways. To show and hide the Inspector window, you can choose View⇨Show Inspector, or you can press ⌘+I, or you can click the circled i button at the lower-left of the project window.

Figure 14-8 shows what the Inspector window looks like when it is focused on the menu displayed in the iDVD window.

Figure 14-8:
Inspecting a
DVD menu.

The Inspector window, in its Menu Info guise, gives you control over these elements of the current theme:

- ✔ **The menu background, including any motion animation:** You can adjust the length of the motion loop and disable or enable any intro or outro that the theme may provide.

- ✔ **The menu audio:** You can set the volume of any audio that's played when the menu is onscreen. You can drag audio from iDVD's Media pane to the audio well in the Inspector window to change the menu audio, and you can drag audio out of the well to remove it.

- ✔ **Menu button placement and appearance:** You can set the highlight color for the active menu button. You can enable or disable the button placement grid that a theme may impose on the menu. The care and feeding of menu buttons is described in Chapter 15.

- ✔ **Drop done visibility:** You can hide all the drop zones, if any, that the theme provides. Because drop zones are merely ornamental menu elements, you might prefer the cleaner look (and lower overhead) of a menu *sans* drop zones.

The media you place in drop zones is one way in which you can customize a menu's theme. Although you can add media to drop zones by dragging items directly to them from the Media browser, that can be difficult if your project employs one of the more complex menu themes that move drop zones onscreen and offscreen during their motion loops. The iDVD drop zone editor, shown in Figure 14-9, was made for such situations.

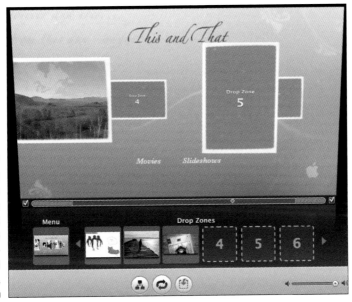

Figure 14-9: The drop zone editor gives access to menu background and drop zones.

 You can show the drop zone editor by clicking the drop zone editor button at the bottom of the project window, or by double-clicking any visible drop zone in the current menu. You can then drag media into or out of the drop zone wells for that menu. As an added bonus, you can also replace the menu background by dragging media (either a still image or a movie) into the menu well in the drop zone editor. Spiffy!

 You can drag the diamond-shaped motion playhead in the scrubber bar below the menu pane to scroll through the animation of any motion menu and bring different drop zones into view (it helps to click the Motion button to turn off menu animation when you scrub through a menu so that the motion playhead stays put). You can also enable or disable menu intros and outros with the check boxes at either side of the bar.

You can drag the following items into a drop zone:

 ✔ **Movies:** The video plays in a loop as long as the menu is visible. Click the drop zone in the menu pane to show the Movie control, as seen in Figure 14-10. You can set the start and end points of a drop zone video with this control. We suggest you choose short video segments for your drop zones: the longer the video, the less room on the DVD for more useful material.

Figure 14-10:
Adjust the
length of a
drop zone
video.

✔ **Photos:** The simplest of media. It just sits there, looking pretty.

✔ **Multiple photos for a slideshow:** The photos play in a slideshow. You can add as many as 99 images to a drop zone. Click the drop zone to see the Photos control (shown in Figure 14-11), which you use to select an initial photo for the slideshow. You can click the Edit Order button in the Photos control to see a simplified slideshow editor (the slideshow editor is described in Chapter 15).

Figure 14-11:
Choose
an initial
image in a
drop zone
slideshow.

If the shape of the drop zone crops the image or video in it, you can hold down ⌘ and drag the media around inside the drop zone to position it to your liking.

Finally, you can change the aspect ratio of the iDVD project to customize the theme. Although each iDVD theme is designed for either a widescreen or a standard aspect ratio, you can switch to the other one: Choose Project⇨Switch to Standard (4:3) or Project⇨Switch to Widescreen (16:9).

The aspect ratio you choose has some implications for any custom background images you may add to a menu. iDVD crops custom background images to fit the exact dimensions of a DVD screen, as follows:

- **Standard:** 720 x 540 (NTSC) or 768 x 576 (PAL)
- **Widescreen:** 854 x 480 (NTSC) or 1024 x 576 (PAL)

TECHNICAL STUFF

PAL? NTSC? These are the two analog video output standards supported by DVDs. NTSC is the standard used in North America and Japan, among other places. PAL is commonly used in most of Europe. PAL and NTSC specify slightly different aspect ratios for both standard and widescreen video.

Saving a Theme

You can save any theme that you've customized (and, truth be told, even those you haven't) as a Favorite, as shown in Figure 14-12. Themes saved as favorites appear in the Themes pane in the project window when you select Favorites from the menu above the Themes list.

Favorites
This and That favorite

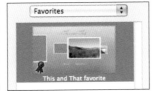

Figure 14-12: One of our favorite things.

REMEMBER

To save a theme as a favorite, choose File⇨Save Theme as Favorite. The dialog shown in Figure 14-13 appears. The favorite's proposed name is the same as the current theme with the word "favorite" appended.

This and That favorite
Shared for all users
Replace existing
Cancel
OK

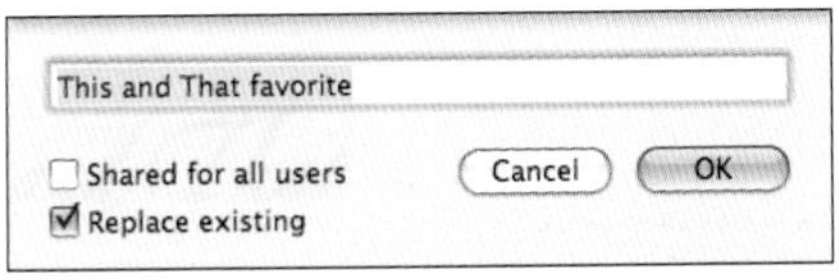

Figure 14-13: Saving a favorite.

Themes you save as favorites are only available from your current user account unless you select the Shared for All Users check box in the dialog shown in Figure 14-13.

By default, if the favorite name you supply matches the name of an existing favorite, the new favorite replaces it and you won't be able to get the older favorite back. You can deselect Replace Existing when you save a favorite to avoid inadvertent obliteration of an existing favorite.

The following items are saved in the favorite theme:

- Customizations to default button and label styles, such as font, color, size, and highlight
- Customizations to the menu background
- Media added to drop zones
- Background audio added to the menu

When you save a favorite, the favorite comprises the current menu only, not the entire theme family. If you have customized different menus in a theme family, you need to save each menu separately.

You can't remove favorites you've saved from within iDVD, but you can find them and drag them to the Trash in the Finder as you would any other file or folder. Favorites saved for your user account are in ~/Library/Application Support/iDVD/Favorites/, as shown in Figure 14-14. Shared favorites reside in /Users/Shared/iDVD/Favorites/ at the top level of your system disk.

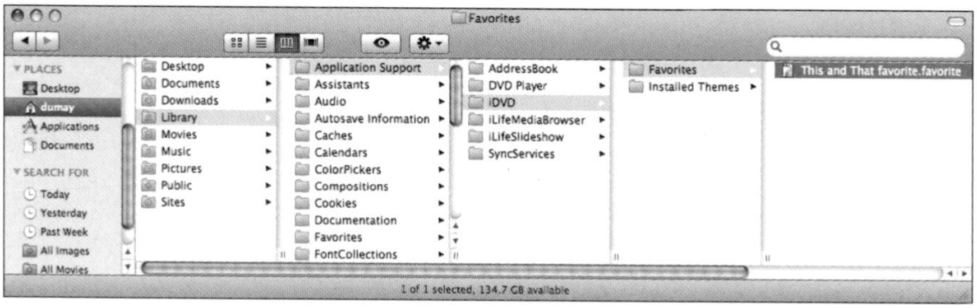

Figure 14-14: We keep our personal favorites in our Library.

15

Assembling Your DVD

In This Chapter

▷ Putting movies on your DVD

▷ Making menu buttons

▷ Preparing a DVD slideshow

▷ Previewing your DVD

*I*n the previous chapter, we covered the themes that control the appearance of your DVD, and you saw how to customize DVD themes so that they look just the way you want. But a DVD without content is like a big tub of popcorn without the popcorn. In this chapter, you find out how to add the crunchy, tasty content that your audience craves: content like movies, slideshows, and menu buttons and text.

Adding DVD Content

As much fun as designing a DVD menu is, menus exist only to provide a way for the audience to find out what stuff is on the DVD, and to provide a way for the audience to play that stuff. That's what menu text and menu buttons are about:

©iStockphoto/Andrey Stratilatov

▹ **Menu buttons:** Menu buttons provide your audience with access to other menus, or to the movies and slideshows on the DVD. Menu buttons can appear as text (most themes use text buttons by default), as text over an ornamental graphic shape, or text with an accompanying thumbnail that represents the material to which the button leads. You add menu buttons by adding movies, slideshows, or submenus to the current menu as described later in this chapter.

✔ **Menu text:** Use menu text to label a menu. Menu text is not dynamic or interactive; it's simply there to be read. Most menu text is very short, and simply describes the menu's contents, or reiterates the name of the DVD itself. Keep in mind that TVs, even high-definition TVs, are not designed for presenting massive quantities of text to the audience. Every menu that you create in iDVD has a default menu text label. You can add additional menu text labels to a menu, if necessary, by choosing Project⇨Add Text, or by pressing ⌘+K.

Adding a movie

You add menu buttons differently from the way you add menu text: to add a menu button, you simply add content to the DVD. When you do, a menu button appears on the current DVD menu to provide access to that content. The most common type of content you add to a DVD is, of course, a movie.

There are several ways to add a movie to a menu:

✔ Click the Add button at the lower left of the project window and choose Add Movie, as shown in Figure 15-1.

Figure 15-1:
One way to add a movie to the current menu.

✔ Choose Project⇨Add Movie, or press Shift+⌘+O.

✔ Drag a movie thumbnail from the Media pane, or from a Finder window, and drop it anywhere on the menu other than in a drop zone.

This last method adds a movie menu button to the menu and automatically links it to the movie that you dragged. The first two methods add the movie menu button to the menu, but you still have to attach an actual movie to it.

You can tell if a movie menu button lacks an associated movie if a small caution icon is present on it, as shown in Figure 15-2.

Figure 15-2:
The caution
icon and
button label
indicates
a movie
button that
lacks a
movie.

This icon means the button lacks an associated movie.

To add a movie to a movie menu button that lacks one, drag a movie either from the Media pane or from a Finder window and drop it on the menu button, as shown in Figure 15-3.

Figure 15-3:
Drag and
drop a
movie on
an unlinked
movie but-
ton to attach
the movie
to it.

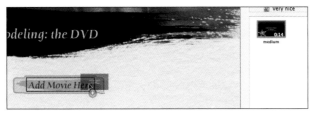

When you add a movie to a movie menu button, the menu button displays the movie name (with one exception, which we describe at the next Remember icon, that involves movies with chapter markers).

When you drag the movie from the Media pane, the menu button label shows the movie name as it appears in the Media pane. When you drag the movie from a Finder window, the menu button label displays the filename of the movie. We describe how to edit the menu button label later in this chapter in the section, "Editing menu text and menu buttons."

iDVD handles movies with chapter markers differently than the way it handles movies without markers. When you add a movie that does not have chapter markers, the menu button links directly to the movie on the final DVD you create: The user selects the menu button and the movie plays. When you add a movie *with* chapter markers, iDVD not only adds the movie, but, by default, adds a scene selection menu as well, although you can turn that behavior off in iDVD's Movie Preferences. The scene selection menu uses the theme family's Chapters theme if the family has one. (Theme families are described in Chapter 14.)

iDVD adds the scene selection menu in different ways depending on how you add a movie to a menu:

- ✔ **If you drop a movie with chapter markers directly on a menu that has no movies, iDVD creates two menu buttons, one labeled Play Movie and the other labeled Scene Selection.** The movie name is not included in either menu button label. The Scene Selection menu button links to a scene selection menu. This menu contains scene menu buttons that play the movie from each chapter marker, as shown in Figure 15-4. Scene selection menus can have as many as six scene menu buttons. If the movie contains more than six chapters, additional scene selection menus are created as needed.

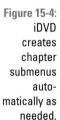

Figure 15-4: iDVD creates chapter submenus auto- matically as needed.

- ✔ **If you drop a movie with chapter markers on a movie menu button that has no attached movie, iDVD labels the menu button with the movie name, as described earlier in this section, and creates a new movie submenu.**

The movie submenu contains Play Movie and Scene Selection menu buttons, as shown in Figure 15-5. The Scene Selection menu button links to the movie's scene selection menu.

We recommend that you add movies using the drag-and-drop method when your project is a simple one, such as one that includes only a single movie with chapters. For projects that include several movies and slideshows, use the Add Movie command: This method gives each movie with chapters its own menu, and thereby helps streamline your DVD's main menu.

Figure 15-5:
A new sub-
menu with
Play Movie
and Scene
Selection
menu
buttons.

Adding a slideshow

DVDs are a great way to share photos with people, and they can be a natural fit with the video on a DVD: for example, a college graduation DVD with both video and still photos, or a student film with a special collection of production stills. iDVD makes photos available as slideshows on the DVD.

You add slideshows to a menu in much the same way as you add movies:

- Click the Add button at the lower left of the project window and choose Add Slideshow.
- Choose Project⇨Add Slideshow or press ⌘+L.
- Drag a group of photos from the Media pane, or from a Finder window, and drop it anywhere on the menu other than in a drop zone.

If you drop an iPhoto Event or iPhoto album, the label on the menu button that leads to the slideshow has the name of the album or Event; otherwise, the menu button label is My Slideshow. We discuss how to change the label and menu button appearance in the next section.

To edit a slideshow, double-click the slideshow menu button. The iDVD slideshow editor, shown in Figure 15-6, appears in place of the current menu. You use the editor to set the slideshow pacing, photo order, accompanying audio, and the transitions between photos.

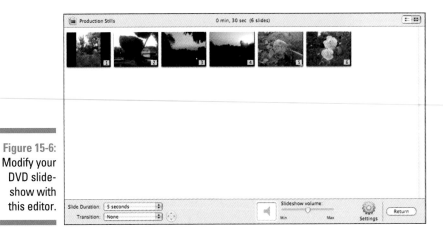

Figure 15-6:
Modify your
DVD slide-
show with
this editor.

You control the order of the slides in the slideshow by dragging the slide thumbnails into place as shown in Figure 15-7.

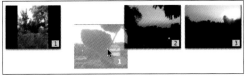

Figure 15-7:
Drag your
slides into
the proper
order.

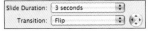

You control the timing and transition effect between slides with the controls at the left of the slideshow editor's toolbar, as shown in more detail in Figure 15-8.

Figure 15-8:
The
timing and
transition
controls.

The Slide Duration menu lets you set how long each slide stays on screen. You can set it for 1, 3, 5, or 10 seconds. You can also set the show to adjust slide durations so that the show lasts exactly as long as the accompanying audio. You give a slideshow accompanying audio by dragging audio from the Media pane to the audio well in the center of the slideshow toolbar (visible at the bottom of Figure 15-6). You can also set the slide duration to be manual, which means that you control when slides change by using the DVD player controls.

The Transition menu provides twelve different transition effects, including flips, reveals, dissolves, and so on. You can also choose to have no transition effect. If an effect involves a spatial move, such as a flip, you can set the direction of the effect with the round four-position controller beside the Transition menu.

The effect you choose controls all of the transitions; you cannot set transition effects on a per-slide basis.

The Settings button at the right of the editor's toolbar brings up the dialog shown in Figure 15-9.

Figure 15-9:
The
slideshow
Settings
dialog.

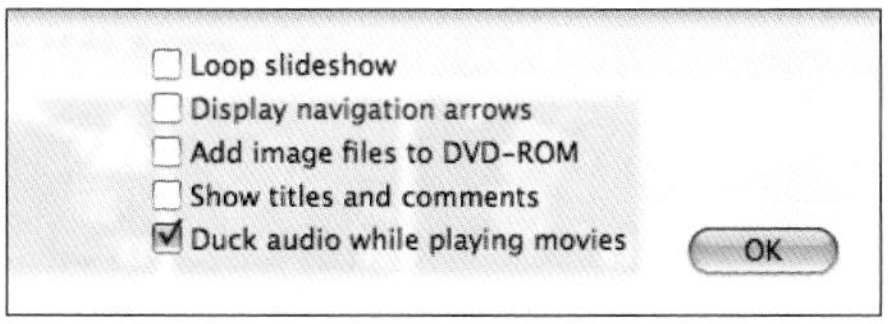

☐ Loop slideshow
☐ Display navigation arrows
☐ Add image files to DVD-ROM
☐ Show titles and comments
☑ Duck audio while playing movies   ⬭ OK ⬭

Here's what the dialog options mean:

- ✔ **Loop Slideshow:** When this is enabled, the slideshow repeats from the beginning after all the slides are shown. This is useful for kiosk applications, parties, or just to waste electricity.

- ✔ **Display Navigation Arrows:** This option superimposes navigation arrows on the TV screen when the slideshow plays. Enable this option when you choose Manual from the Slide Duration menu.

- ✔ **Add Image Files to DVD-ROM:** Enable this option to have iDVD set aside a portion of the DVD's storage for files that you can access on a computer, and to put the original photo files that make up the slideshow in that storage space. This allows the recipient of the DVD, for example, to print the photos in their original resolution.

✔ **Show Titles and Comments:** If you have added titles or comments to the photos in iPhoto, they appear superimposed on the photos when the slideshow plays if this is selected. You can also see and edit the titles and comments in the slideshow editor.

✔ **Duck Audio While Playing Movies:** If the album or Events you drag to the editor include video, enable this to have any accompanying audio in the slideshow lower its volume when a video clip plays.

After you finish editing a slideshow, click Return at the right of the editor toolbar to close the editor.

Editing menu text and menu buttons

You can edit both the appearance and the text labels of menu text and of menu buttons.

To edit menu text (as opposed to the text label of a menu button), double-click the text label. If the Inspector window is not open, a simple in-place formatting control appears adjacent to the label, as shown in Figure 15-10.

Figure 15-10:
Double-click a menu text label to edit and format it.

Open the Inspector window: You can choose View↵Show Inspector, or press ⌘+I, or click the Inspector button at the lower left of the iDVD project window. The Inspector window provides more text formatting options, as shown in Figure 15-11.

Figure 15-11:
The Inspector window provides more extensive text formatting.

You can edit the text labels of menu buttons, but *not* by double-clicking the label. Instead, to select menu button label text for editing, you click the menu button once to select it, and then pause, and then click again on the text. Why? Because double-clicking a menu button does something else, depending on the type of menu button you double-click:

- ✔ **Menu button linked to a submenu:** A double-click displays the submenu.

- ✔ **Menu button linked to a movie:** A double-click opens a preview of the movie in the iDVD preview player (we discuss previewing a DVD later in this chapter).

- ✔ **Menu button linked to a slideshow:** A double-click opens the slideshow editor, described earlier in this chapter.

In our very humble opinions (and we take pride in our humility), using the same mouse gesture to do four *completely different things* is very confusing. It's even *more* confusing when the objects you double-click can, and often do, look exactly like each other on the screen. The double-click quadruple entendre in iDVD brings new meaning to the phrase "counter-intuitive."

When no Inspector window is open, a click-pause-click on a menu button displays the same kind of in-place formatting control for the menu button's label that was shown previously in Figure 15-10. If an Inspector window is open (and remember, a simple ⌘+I opens it), you see advanced formatting options in that window.

The formatting options you see in the Inspector window depend on the menu button's style, which can be one of the following:

- ✔ **Text menu button:** When not selected, the button appears as text. This is the default style of most menu buttons in most theme families. The Inspector window for a text menu button is shown in Figure 15-12.

Figure 15-12: Inspecting a text menu button.

✔ **Image menu button:** The menu button displays an image or a video loop inside a frame in addition to the menu button's label. Figure 15-13 shows the Inspector window for an image menu button.

Figure 15-13:
Complete formatting options for an image menu button.

✔ **Shape menu button:** In most cases, a shape menu button looks just like a text menu button, but uses a shape to highlight the button when the user selects it with the DVD control, as shown in Figure 15-14. Some shape buttons also have a second shape that always appears with the menu button, whether highlighted or not. The Inspector window for a shape menu button looks like Figure 15-13, but without the Movie slider and Custom thumbnail well.

Figure 15-14:
A shape menu button with a high-light shape visible.

You set the menu button style with the pop-up menu above the Buttons pane, as shown in Figure 15-15. The first three items on the menu (yes, even the first item, Text) show you the available categories of highlight shapes for shape menu buttons. The other items provide categories of frames for image menu buttons.

Figure 15-15:
Highlight
and frame
categories
for menu
buttons.

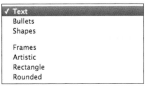

Here are the things you can control about a menu button's appearance with
the Inspector window:

- **Font, size, style, text alignment, color, and shadow:** The controls for
  adjusting these appear at the top of the Inspector window, regardless of
  the menu button style.

- **Image displayed:** You can drag any image, group of images, or movie to
  the Custom thumbnail well to apply a custom image to an image menu
  button. You use the Thumbnail slider to select which image the menu
  button displays. This gets tricky, however, because the media you drop
  in the well is added to any other available images for that menu button.
  For example, a menu button for a slideshow can show slides from the
  slideshow as well as the images you add to the well. Even more tricky,
  if you add a movie to the Custom thumbnail well for a slideshow menu
  button, the movie plays when you select it with the Thumbnail slider,
  which might give the audience the impression that the button links to a
  movie and not a slideshow.

  Our advice: Don't add custom thumbnails to image menu buttons that
  link to slideshows or to movies because you'll only get confused, and
  you may confuse your audience as well. You can remove the custom
  image or video by dragging it out of the well.

- **Movie loop or still image:** When an image menu button links to a movie,
  the menu button displays the linked movie in its frame. You can use the
  Movie slider in the Inspector to set where in the movie the loop for the
  movie begins. The length of the loop is the length of the menu's motion
  loop, which we discuss in Chapter 14. To display a still image from the
  movie instead of a loop, select the Still Image check box, and then use
  the Movie slider to select the frame to display.

- **Size of the image frame or highlight shape:** The Size slider adjusts how
  big the frame is for an image menu button, or the size of the highlight
  (and decorative background graphic, if any) for a shape menu button.

- **Label position:** For shape or image menu buttons, you can use the Label
  menu to set where the highlight, background, or image frame appear
  relative to the menu button's label text.

✔ **Transition effect when the menu button is chosen:** The two Transition menus set the video effect shown when the user chooses a menu button to go to another menu or to see a movie or slideshow. The top Transition menu provides a choice of transition effects, and the bottom menu provides the direction in which the transition effect plays (such as left or right) — that is, if a direction is applicable to the chosen transition effect. For example, a dissolve has no direction, but a wipe does.

 To remove the highlight shape or image frame from a menu button, choose the first item that appears in the Button pane (you can see in the margin what the item looks like). Choosing this item, in essence, applies the text menu button style to the menu button. To reset the menu button's appearance to the style specified by the theme, Control-click or right-click the menu button and choose Reset to Theme.

Previewing your DVD content

As we noted previously, double-clicking a menu button linked to a movie opens the iDVD preview player, which then proceeds to play the movie. That's fine if you just want to preview a movie that's part of your project, but it doesn't give you the complete DVD-viewing experience, with its animated motion menus and the ability to navigate between menus.

Here's how to preview your complete DVD project:

1. **Navigate to the main menu in your project.**

   This step is optional; the preview function begins at the current menu in the project window. Starting the preview at the main menu gives you a better feel for how the DVD presents itself.

2. **Click the Preview button.**

   This button lies in the toolbar below the menu editing pane, as shown in Figure 15-16. When you click it, the project window is replaced by the preview player window and the DVD remote control, as shown in Figure 15-17.

Figure 15-16:
The Preview button lives between the volume slider and the Burn button.

Preview button

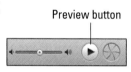

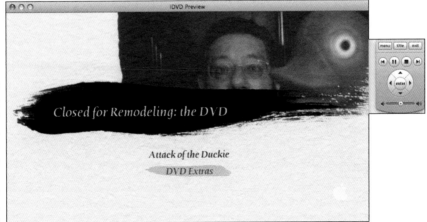

Figure 15-17:
The preview
player is
accompa-
nied by its
own DVD
remote
control.

3. **Click the controls in the DVD remote control window (Figure 15-18) to navigate and to play the DVD:**

   • **Menu:** This ends playback of a movie or slideshow and returns to the menu from which it started.

   • **Title:** This displays the DVD's main menu.

   • **Exit:** This ends the preview.

   • **Player controls:** These provide the previous chapter, pause, play, and next chapter commands, respectively, for viewing movies and slideshows.

   • **Round directional control:** The arrow buttons on the control move the highlight around the current menu. The Enter button in the center selects the currently highlighted menu button.

   • **Volume slider:** You can probably guess what this does.

4. **In the remote control, click Exit.**

   This ends the preview and brings back the project window. You can also end the preview by clicking the close button at the top left of the preview window.

Figure 15-18:
The remote
control
window.

The iDVD volume control is relative to your Mac's system-wide volume setting. In other words, if your Mac's volume is set to 50 percent, an iDVD volume of 50 percent gives you 25 percent of the possible Mac volume. So, if you have your Mac's volume set low, no amount of fiddling with the iDVD volume slider is going to raise the volume very much.

Playing it safe

In addition to previewing the DVD, you also should check the TV Safe Area and, for widescreen DVDs, the Standard Crop Area.

The TV Safe Area shows you the parts of the screen that may not be visible on TVs that have picture tubes; picture tubes, if not precisely calibrated (and most are not), don't display the complete video image from edge to edge. Most professional TV camera operators have the safe area marked on their camera viewfinders to help them frame shots that can be seen on all TVs, regardless of calibration. Choose View⇨Show TV Safe Area or press ⌘+T to see it.

The Standard Crop Area shows the part of a widescreen DVD that falls outside the boundaries of a standard aspect ratio TV screen. To see it, choose View⇨Show Standard Crop Area, or press Option+⌘+T. Naturally, if your project uses a standard aspect ratio, the Show Standard Crop Area command is not available.

Both areas are shown in Figure 15-19; the TV Safe Area is the inner red rectangle. iDVD's themes always try to position menu buttons and menu labels within the TV Safe Area. However, you can drag menu buttons around to override the theme's menu button placement, so it helps to know if the menu buttons are visible where you put them.

Figure 15-19:
The TV Safe Area (inner rectangle) and Standard Crop Area (outer rectangle).

Closed for Remodeling: the DVD

Attack of the Duckie
DVD Extras

To restore menu buttons to where the theme wants them, bring up the Inspector window for the menu (⌘+I) and click Snap to Grid in the Buttons area of the Inspector window.

Managing DVD Menus

You can build iDVD projects that have rather elaborate menu structures. For example, suppose you teach a media class, and you want to showcase five student videos, along with production slideshows for each video. You can easily add menus for each student's video and other material with the Add Submenu command. This command is available on the project window's Add button, as shown back in Figure 15-1. You can also issue the command by choosing Project➪Add Submenu (Shift+⌘+N).

When you create a new submenu, iDVD uses the theme family's Extras theme, if there is one, and places a menu button on the current menu to link to it. The submenu starts out empty, but you can add movies, slideshows, and even other submenus to it.

Figure 15-20 shows a typical submenu, with a couple of menu buttons on it. Each submenu that you create automatically includes a menu button that links to the main menu; in Figure 15-20, it's the brush-stroke styled left arrow near the bottom left.

Figure 15-20: A submenu with some extras added.

A menu button that links to the main menu.

To help your audience get around a DVD menu structure that may go many levels deep, you can also add a Title menu button to any menu other than the first one. When your audience selects a title button, the DVD displays its title menu, which is, by convention, the very first menu. To create a title menu button, choose Project⇨Add Title Menu Button.

As you build your project, there's also a tool to help *you* get around a DVD menu structure that may go many levels deep: the DVD Map, which you can access with the DVD Map button (shown in the margin) on the project window's toolbar. Figure 15-21 shows the DVD Map for a project.

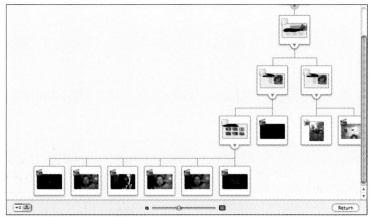

Figure 15-21:
Your DVD treasure map.

Each square on the map represents a menu, a slideshow, or a movie. You can use the slider at the bottom of the map to zoom in or out of the map, and you can choose either a horizontal or vertical map layout with the control at the left of the toolbar. The Return button closes the DVD map and returns you to the last menu that was displayed in the project window.

You can double-click any item in the map with the following results:

   ✔ **Menu:** The DVD map is replaced by that menu in the project window.

   ✔ **Slideshow:** The slideshow editor for that slideshow opens. When you click Return in the editor, you return to the DVD map.

   ✔ **Movie:** The movie plays in the preview viewer. When you close the viewer, you return to the DVD map.

You can also move both menus and media around in the DVD map. Just drag an item, either media or a menu, on top of a menu in the map to move it to that menu. Figure 15-22 shows a slideshow being moved from a submenu to the main menu of a project.

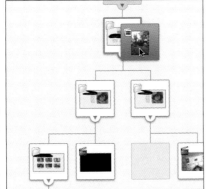

Figure 15-22: Moving menus on the map.

One of the easiest things to do with a menu, movie, or slideshow is to delete it. You can select the menu button that leads to it and press Delete, or you can select it in the DVD map and press Delete. Either way, it disappears with a satisfying puff of smoke. Keep in mind, however, that any movies, slide-shows, or submenus belonging to a menu that you delete are also deleted.

Adding DVD-ROM Content

One part of the DVD that your audience never sees on their TV sets is the optional DVD-ROM area of the DVD. You can put any files you like on your DVD, which turns it into a DVD-ROM. The DVD still plays in an ordinary DVD player, but the files you add become available when you insert the DVD into a computer's optical disc reader.

In the section titled, "Adding a slideshow" earlier this chapter, we mentioned how you can include a slideshow's original photos on a DVD: Through an iDVD preference setting. The way you add other files to the DVD-ROM is as follows:

1. **Choose Advanced⇨Edit DVD-ROM Contents.**

   The window shown in Figure 15-23 appears.

DVD-ROM Contents	
Name	Size
▶ 📁 Slideshows	46 MB

(New Folder) (Add Files...)

Figure 15-23:
Add some
files to your
DVD.

2. **Drag files or folders from the Finder into the window.**

You can also click Add Files and choose files to add from a dialog.

You can delete files or folders from the DVD-ROM contents by selecting them in the DVD-ROM Contents window and pressing Delete. When you are done adding files to or removing files from the DVD-ROM, just close the DVD-ROM Contents window.

16

Burning Your DVD

*I*t's been a long road, getting from there, when footage was sitting on your digital video camera, to here, when you're ready to create a DVD to distribute your movie. But now, at last, your journey leaves the realm of pixels and packets and enters the realm of the real. Now is when you finally produce something that you can actually hold in the palm of your hand, a shiny rainbow-hued objet d'art.

In this chapter, we show you how to burn a DVD.

Burning a DVD Disc

Burning a DVD may be the simplest part of the whole movie-making process. It's certainly the one that requires the least amount of creative thought and energy. However, because the process can consume hours, you do want to get it right the first time: After the DVD is burned, you can't "fix it in post-production" like they do in Hollywood.

©Corbis Digital Stock

Preflighting your project

Before you click the closed-shutter icon at the bottom of your project window to start burning your DVD, you should take heed of the carpenter's idiom: "Measure twice, cut once." Here's a short checklist you can use to make sure your DVD project is ready to burn:

✔ **Check the DVD map:** iDVD puts warnings on the menu thumbnails in your project's DVD map (described in Chapter 15) when it detects that something is not quite right, such as a menu with no buttons, or a drop-zone that contains no media. If you see warnings on the map, resolve them.

✔ **Preview everything in your DVD project:** We explained how to preview your DVD in Chapter 15; now is the time to do it. Preview each of the movies and slideshows in your project to make sure that they play completely from beginning to the end. Click each of your menu buttons to make sure that they go to the right place. Adjust the volume of menu background audio (described in Chapter 14) to make sure that playback isn't too loud in comparison to your movie's audio. Double-check everything before you turn the lasers loose on your recordable DVD.

✔ **Check the power:** If you are going to be burning the DVD on a MacBook, plug it in. You really don't want to run out of battery power midway through the burning process, and the burning process can suck up battery power very quickly.

✔ **Make sure you have enough disk space:** The amount of space you need to have available on your disk drive should be double the amount the final DVD requires. You can find out how big your DVD will be by looking at the Project Info window, described in the next section. If your DVD project is stored on your system disk, you should also make sure that you have additional space available for Mac OS X to use — about ten percent of the total system disk size is a reasonable minimum.

✔ **Have a spare recordable disc or two on hand:** This is a just-in-case tip — occasionally recordable DVD media isn't perfect (shocking, we know). If iDVD reports a disc recording error, you don't want to have to drop everything and run out to buy a new blank disc.

✔ **Make sure you have plenty of time:** As we discuss in the later section, "Choosing the Encoder," burning a DVD can take many hours. You don't need to baby-sit your Mac while it works, but you shouldn't plan to burn a DVD when you'll be needing your Mac for other important tasks. When your Mac is burning a DVD, that is its most important task, and it can't be interrupted as it works.

✔ **Make sure your encoding settings are appropriate:** We discuss that in more detail in the next section because it's a crucial part of making a DVD.

Choosing the encoder

Encoding converts the media you have added to your project into the format that the DVD standard requires. The details of the standard are not important (although we touched the tip of that iceberg back in Chapter 12). What is important is that the encoder setting you choose for your project determines how much material you can put on the DVD, how long it takes to burn the DVD, and how good the results look when you play the finished DVD.

iDVD helps you out with the first part — how much material you can put on the DVD — when you open your project. If you have put more material into your project than can fit on a DVD using the current project settings, iDVD displays a dialog like the one shown in Figure 16-1.

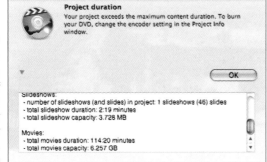

Figure 16-1: This dialog appears if your media is bigger than your disc.

Figure 16-2 shows the Project Info window to which that dialog refers. To see the Project Info window, choose Project⇨Project Info, or press Shift+⌘+I.

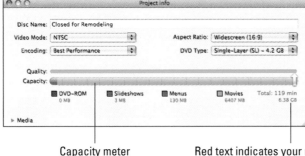

Figure 16-2: Here's where you set the encoder and DVD type for your DVD project.

Capacity meter   Red text indicates your movie is too large for the current encoding and/or DVD type.

You can see how much disc space a project requires under the Capacity meter in the Project Info window. When the disc space amount appears in red, as it does in Figure 16-2, it means you have to choose a different encoder or set a different disc type. (The disc type is set with the DVD Type pop-up menu on the right side of the Project window: Macs with older optical drives can burn only single-layer discs, but newer Macs with SuperDrive optical drives can burn both single-layer and double-layer discs.)

You set the encoder with the Encoding pop-up menu at the left of the window. It offers the following three encoders:

- **Best Performance:** This is the default encoder. The name refers to how much processing time your Mac devotes to encoding, not to how well the video plays after it's encoded. The Best Performance encoder is the only encoder that can do its work in the background while you work on your iDVD project (although you can turn background encoding off by choosing Advanced⇨Encode in Background). Best Performance encoding can fit about an hour's worth of video on a single-layer DVD, and about two hours on a double-layer DVD. Although this encoder can fit less material on a DVD than the two other encoders can, the picture quality is always good, as you can see from the Quality meter shown in Figure 16-2.

- **High Quality:** This encoder uses more processing power, and spends more time encoding, than the Best Performance encoder. It does this in order to try to fit as much material as possible on the DVD. This encoder trades picture quality for disc space if necessary: it can fit about two hours of video on a single-layer DVD, and about four hours on a double-layer DVD.

  Figure 16-3 shows a part of the Project Info window for a project that uses the High Quality setting to fit almost two hours of video on a single-layer DVD: Note that the Quality meter indicates deep orange for the amount of material being encoded, indicating that the picture quality will be reduced. Projects that use the High Quality encoder can take several hours to encode and burn a DVD.

Figure 16-3:
Stuffing too much material on a DVD can reduce picture quality.

The orange color indicates quality will be compromised.

- **Professional Quality:** This encoder uses even more processing power, and spends even more time encoding, than does the High Quality encoder. It can fit the same amount of material on a DVD as the High Quality encoder can, but it produces better looking results. The Professional Quality encoder can take twice as long to encode the same material as the High Quality encoder. If you're going to burn a full double-layer DVD, bring a good book or two to read, or schedule a family outing, because your Mac is going to be spending half a day or more encoding your project.

Feeling the burn

You've done the preflight check. You've set the encoder and disc type for the project. You've got the blank DVD media in hand.

Now here's what you do:

1. **Click the burn button at the bottom of the iDVD project window, or choose File⇨Burn DVD (⌘+R).**

   The burn button looks like a closed shutter until you click it, whereupon it becomes the familiar rotating radioactive burn symbol shown in the margin. iDVD prompts you to insert a recordable DVD disc.

2. **Insert a blank DVD into your Mac's optical drive.**

   Your Mac spends a few moments detecting the disc, and then presents you with the dialog shown in Figure 16-4. This dialog keeps you posted on what iDVD is doing at each stage of the DVD creation process. The time estimate you see may be inaccurate at the beginning of the process, but in just a couple of minutes, the estimate stabilizes and tends to be reliable.

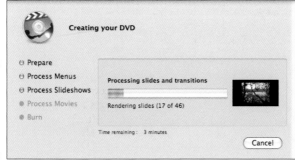

Figure 16-4: iDVD lets you know what's going on.

Keep in mind that if you use the Best Performance encoder and if iDVD has managed to encode all of the video in the background before you began burning your DVD, the Process Movies stage goes by very quickly. On the other hand, if you use either of the other two encoders, the Process Movies stage takes the bulk of the estimated time shown.

3. **Take note of the time remaining and step away from the keyboard.**

   Plan to return to your Mac when the DVD creation process finishes. When iDVD completes its work, it ejects the finished disc and then presents you with the dialog shown in Figure 16-5.

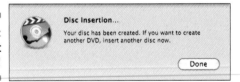

Figure 16-5:
Let's do it
again!

4. **Either insert another blank DVD and burn a second DVD, or click Done.**

Because iDVD encodes everything in your project when it performs a burn, burning a second copy immediately afterward takes much less time: In fact, iDVD only needs the time required to physically burn the DVD. So if you want a second copy of your masterpiece, now's the best time to do it.

Congratulations: You have become a DVD mastering . . . well . . . master. Find yourself a DVD player, or stick your finished masterpiece back in your Mac (see Figure 16-6) and fire up the Mac's DVD player. It's movie time! Pass the popcorn.

Figure 16-6:
The finished
product,
ready to
play.

Making and Burning a DVD Disc Image

If you don't happen to have any blank discs on hand, or if you think you might want to burn additional copies of your DVD from time to time, you can make a disc image instead of burning your project directly to disc. Then after you have the disc image, you can use your Mac's Disk Utility application to burn a new a disc every time you want another copy of your DVD.

iDVD can only create a single-layer DVD disc image reliably; double-layer disc images can be created with iDVD, but the discs made from these images may not work in many DVD players. If your project requires a dual-layer DVD, you should burn it directly from iDVD.

The process of making a DVD image is almost identical to the process of burning a disc. Just choose File⇨Save as Disc Image, and specify a file location in the dialog that appears. iDVD then goes through the same creation steps it does when you actually burn a DVD and then stores the image where you requested.

After you have created a disc image, you burn DVDs from it with Disk Utility, which is located in /Applications/Utilities/. Here's how to burn a DVD with Disk Utility:

1. **Open Disk Utility.**

   The Disk utility window is shown in Figure 16-7.

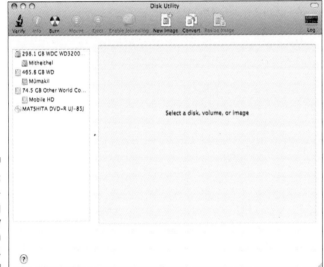

Figure 16-7:
The un-
assuming
Disk Utility
application
window.

2. **On the Disk Utility toolbar, click Burn.**

   Disk Utility presents you with a standard file dialog.

3. **Navigate to the location of the disc image file, select the file, and then click Burn.**

   Disk Utility presents a dialog asking you to insert a disc. If you like, you can click the arrow button in the upper right of the dialog to see detailed burning options, as shown in Figure 16-8.

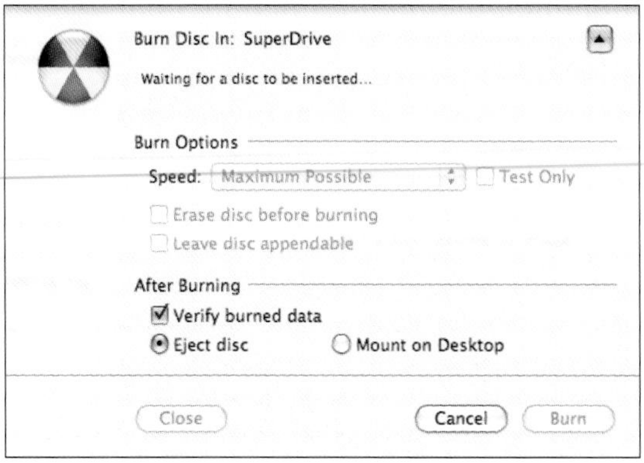

Figure 16-8:
Disk Utility
has some
burning
options.

4. Insert a disc, wait until Disk Utility recognizes the disc, and then click Burn.

Disk Utility shows you a progress dialog as it burns the disc.

5. When the burn is complete, choose Disk Utility⇨Quit.

That's all, folks! Roll the credits.

Part V
The Part of Tens

The 5th Wave   By Rich Tennant

"Why don't you try blurring the brimstone and then putting a nice glow effect around the hellfire."

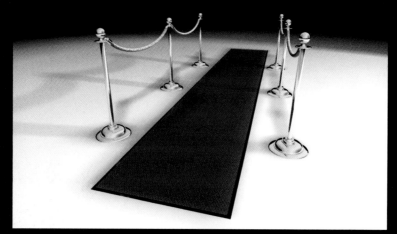

© iStockphoto/Sean Locke

In this part . . .

In this Part, we provide two chapters that are a Dummies tradition: "Part of Tens" chapters.

Chapter 17 discusses 10 hardware and software items that we think can benefit you when working with iMovie and iDVD to produce your movies. It focuses on items that range in price from free to less than $200.

Chapter 18 lists 10 tips and techniques you can employ when using iMovie and iDVD.

Ten Useful Hardware and Software Add-ons

*J*ohn Donne wrote, "No man is an island, entire unto himself." iMovie and iDVD aren't men, but neither are they islands. Like any of us, they can sometimes use a helping hand. We aren't going to belabor the obvious pieces of hardware that help you with your work, such as a good digital camcorder, a tripod, a microphone for your camera, or a DVD burner — that would be tantamount to cheating. In this chapter, we focus on ten items that we think are great companions for iMovie and iDVD.

EyeTV

Elgato (www.elgato.com) makes and supports the award-winning EyeTV hardware and software. Most famous as a way to view and record TV on your Mac, EyeTV also gives you a way to get old, non-digital video and audio onto your Mac from a Beta or VHS player, old-fashioned analog camcorder, or a cassette tape deck or turntable, as long as it has composite plug capability (composite plugs are those red and white RCA plugs for stereo, with a yellow plug for video). EyeTV offers numerous models, from the EyeTV Hybrid, which uses your Mac's processor to encode

©iStockphoto/Wil Fernandez

the video, to the EyeTV 250 Plus, which encodes the video before sending it on to your Mac's hard disk.

Elgato makes moving your content from VHS tape easy by providing the VHS Assistant. Just choose Help⇨EyeTV VHS Assistant or, if you want the video encoded for the iPod or iPhone, choose Help⇨EyeTV iPod Assistant. In either case, just follow the onscreen instructions as EyeTV walks you through the process. When done, the EyeTV software exports your recording to iTunes. You can retrieve it from there by choosing File⇨Import⇨Movies and navigating to your ~/Music/iTunes/iTunes Music/Movies folder, where you find the .m4v file(s) you've created. Select your recording and click Import. iMovie creates a new Event consisting of your recording.

Alternatively, you can manually manage the AV import process in EyeTV without using either Assistant.

Whether you record manually or use an assistant, your recordings are also in the EyeTV software's Library under Recordings. You can export manually, directly to iMovie, by selecting the recording and choosing File⇨Export and choosing for iMovie '09 from the Format pop-up menu, as shown in Figure 17-1.

If you want a device specifically attuned to working with your camcorder and creating video for your iPod, iPhone, or AppleTV, the Turbo.264 HD ($149.95 list price) might be just the ticket. It's small, fast, and easy to use.

Figure 17-1:
Exporting
from EyeTV
to iMovie.

MPEG Streamclip

We don't know about you, but sometimes we receive video files from friends or family that aren't in a form that iMovie accepts. However, if the movie can be opened in QuickTime (even with the use of a codec such as DivX or Perian), MPEG Streamclip (www.squared5.com) can let you export to a wide variety of formats, many of which are iMovie-compatible. Check out Figure 17-2 to see some of the formats to which MPEG Streamclip can export. Best of all, it's free.

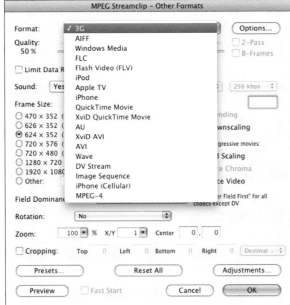

Figure 17-2:
MPEG
Streamclip
helps you
convert
to iMovie-
compatible
formats.

Toast Titanium

iDVD is great for authoring beautiful DVDs, but whether you burn your movie in iDVD or use Disk Utility to burn a saved image file, you have to go through a whole sequence of steps for each copy you want to burn. When we create a family movie that needs to go out to a variety of friends and relatives (for example, a holiday DVD that augments or replaces the traditional year-end holiday letter), we need lots of copies. Toast Titanium (www.roxio.com) fills the bill. Just load the image file and let Toast know how many copies you want to burn. Then, all you have to do is sit there and replace finished burns with blank discs until the job is done.

TIP

If that were the only thing we used Toast for, it probably wouldn't be worth the price tag. But Toast is excellent for creating quick DVD, SuperVideoCDs, and VideoCDs, as well as DivX discs that play in many modern DVD players — not to mention data discs in a variety of formats and audio discs.

Although the menus aren't as fancy as those in iDVD, you have more control over the encoding process with Toast, so if you really want to fit more than two hours of DVD video on a single-layer DVD-R, Toast is your way to accomplish the goal. You can also create a dual-layer image file in iDVD and then have Toast compress it to fit on a single-layer disc. Your movie will deteriorate slightly in quality, but it probably won't be noticeable except in high-speed action scenes, and you'll still have the menus that you so painstakingly created in iDVD. Toast 10 Titanium's Video pane is shown in Figure 17-3.

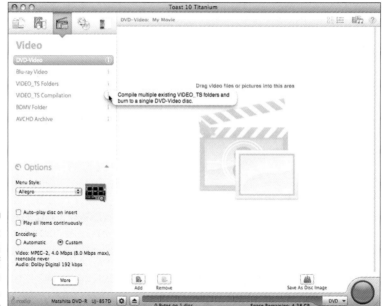

Figure 17-3:
Toast burns
lots of
video disc
formats.

Figure 17-3 also displays the tooltip for one of our favorite features. We burn a lot of DVDs for family that have only one or two short movies on them. You know the type: little Marcus's birthday party or Taylor's graduation or a vacation slideshow. Of course, we have to get copies of these out to all interested family members as soon as possible. When all is said and done, we end up with 10 or 12 DVDs a year, the combined content of which wouldn't even fill one DVD. Rather than having to build an all-new DVD in iDVD, redoing the menus, and reimporting and reencoding the video, Toast lets us select copies of the VIDEO_TS folders (see Chapter 18) from all the DVDs. It then compiles them for us into an all-new, all-encompassing VIDEO_TS folder and burns it to DVD. If you used Magic DVD or One-Step DVD a few times, this feature lets you combine those into one DVD as well. Cool!

And if all that isn't enough to whet your appetite, you also get the capability of writing Blu-ray discs (with a suitable Blu-ray burner), giving you a way to use your HD camera content in a high-def setting (iDVD doesn't do HD).

An External Hard Drive

The glamorous people say that you can't be too rich or too thin (though we might argue the latter). At least as true is this: You can never have too much disk space. Digital video consumes hard disk space the way kids consume Halloween candy. iMovie and iDVD both like a lot of available disk space with which to work, and OS X runs a lot faster when there's a lot of free space for swap files. Get a large fast hard drive and dedicate it to your video, leaving your startup drive's space to OS X: You'll be glad you did. You can find excellent name-brand drives with 1TB (terabyte) or more space for under $300 these days, and the prices keep falling as the capacities increase. (You've gotta love electronics . . . it's one of the very few product lines where you keep getting more and more for the same or less money each year.)

iDVD ThemePAKs

Apple supplies a plethora of menu themes for iDVD, but we often don't find one that meets our needs and we end up having to customize it. iDVD ThemePAKs (www.idvdthemepak.com) offer dozens of iDVD themes that you can plug in and use. Although most are nominally priced and bundle deals are available, you can even download a free package of seven themes.

A bundle of 42 custom menu buttons for use with iDVD is also available for $74.

iMovieLocationEditor

New Zealand's Craig Stanton (craig.stanton.net.nz/code/imovie locationeditor) provides a free utility that lets you easily add locations to the 1,600 Apple put on iMovie's globe. Locations are covered in Chapter 8.

You can type the new locations in by hand or (our preference) copy them from Google Earth.

Direct CD/DVD Printer

When you author a DVD to share with friends and family, go the extra mile and design the stylish label your opus deserves, or just do it for yourself. Many printers, including models from Epson and HP, can print directly to printable CDs and DVDs. Printable discs cost only a penny or two more than regular optical discs if you shop around a bit. That's less than the per-label cost of a pack of press-on disc labels and you don't have to worry about applying the label "just right."

Alternatively, you could invest in a LightScribe external DVD burner. Although this saves considerably on the most expensive aspect of printing — ink — the incremental blank disc cost makes it pretty much a wash, and LightScribe doesn't give you the colorful label that printing affords. That said, Dennis has a LightScribe-compatible burner (a LaCie), but has only burned a handful of LightScribe discs versus thousands of printable DVDs and CDs. If you're going to purchase an external burner, you might make the investment in a LightScribe-compatible one, just in case.

An External Tray-Loading DVD Burner

If you're going to burn a lot of DVDs or if you have a USB camcorder that writes to a miniDVD, you really want a tray-loading drive, and the only current Mac model that sports one internally is the Mac Pro. You can't load a miniDVD in a slot-loading drive, so your only access to what you've recorded is through iMovie's import functionality. A slot-loading drive, the ones used in every Mac except the MacPro, slurps the disc in, a tray loader extends a tray onto which you place your disc and then press the close button (either in software or on the drive case) to retract the tray. In addition to this increased capability, tray-loading drives are faster and, in our experience, last longer than slot-loaders. Further, when they do die, they're a lot easier and less expensive to replace.

A USB Microphone

This recommendation isn't for your camcorder; it's for your Mac. You can use the built-in microphone or iSight camera for your narrations, and they're adequate. But, is "adequate" what you want for your movie? A quality USB-based microphone makes recording your narration much easier because you don't have to position yourself "just so" in order to obtain a consistent recording. Additionally, it's useful if you choose to add a voice track to a GarageBand score for your movie.

An iPod or an iPhone

These portable players are awesome for carrying your video library around and showing it off. Although the screens are small, the video is clear and crisp. Plus, with the appropriate cable, you can connect your iPod to a TV set or home entertainment center and share your video artistry without having to deal with a stack of clumsy DVDs.

Ten Tips and Troubleshooting Hints

We spend the bulk of this book taking you through the basic tools and techniques for making movies and putting them on DVDs. In this chapter, we give you ten tips and troubleshooting tricks that can give your creative endeavors an extra power-assist.

Moving an iDVD Project

If you ever need to move an iDVD project to a different computer or make a complete backup of it, you can pack up all the bits and pieces by choosing File⇨Archive Project and choosing a place to save your project. The Archive Project dialog shows you how big the archive will be and allows you to include both customized themes and any encoded video. Your archive contains all the movies, audio, photos, themes, and all of the files you've included in the DVD-ROM contents. The only thing that won't be in the archive are any special fonts you may have used in your menus.

©iStockphoto/Andrew Johnson

You can then copy the archived project to another computer and open it there with iDVD's File⇨Open command, just as you would any other iDVD project.

Changing Default Clip Click Behavior

By default, when you click a clip in iMovie's Events library, iMovie selects a four-second-long chunk of the clip. You can adjust the size of the chunk you select when you click, or even change what a click means. Choose iMovie⇨Preferences and then click Browser. In the Browser preferences, you can use the slider at the bottom to adjust how much a click selects, or you can choose to make a click select the entire clip — or, instead, have a click deselect everything.

Previewing Your Video with a Video_TS Folder

In Chapter 16, we cover how to make a DVD disc image. However, you don't need a disc image to make a version of your DVD's contents that you can play with your Mac's DVD Player application or other applications that can play DVDs. Instead, you can save a VIDEO_TS folder, using File⇨Save as VIDEO_TS folder. (A VIDEO_TS is the folder on the DVD that contains all the goodies that a DVD player plays.)

Although a VIDEO_TS folder takes almost as much time to make as an actual DVD, it does have certain advantages. Here's one of the most important: It's an excellent way to check the video quality produced by the encoding settings you've chosen for your DVD without using up a blank disc. Although you can't make a DVD from a VIDEO_TS folder with iDVD, you can with other products, such as Toast (see Chapter 17).

Here's how you can view the VIDEO_TS folder with your Mac's DVD Player application: just drag and drop the folder on your Mac's DVD Player application, or choose File⇨Open DVD Media in the DVD Player application and select the VIDEO_TS folder you saved. It will play just like any other DVD on your Mac.

Putting a Happy Face on Your Titles

When you edit a title in your iMovie project, clicking the Show Fonts button in the Viewer brings up a Choose Font dialog that offers nine fonts and colors from which you can choose. Although you can choose other fonts via the System Font Panel button in the dialog, that can be a drag if there's a particular font or two that you always want available.

You can specify the fonts, and the available colors, that appear in the Choose Fonts dialog by choosing iMovie⇨Preferences and then clicking Fonts. Click the double-arrows to the right of a font name to choose a different font to appear in the Choose Font dialog (see Figure 18-1). Click a color swatch to see the Color Picker, from which you can select a color to replace the color in the swatch.

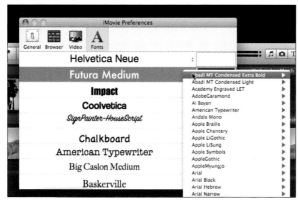

Figure 18-1:
Pick a font,
any font.

Keeping Names Consistent

iDVD uses the name you gave your DVD to name the DVD it creates. And, as we mention in Chapter 16, you can change that name in the Project Info window. However, the disc name may not exactly match the project name, and it may not match the name that you enter in the Project Info window. That's because the DVD standard has specific rules for DVD names.

A DVD can't have names longer than 27 characters, and the name can only include upper-case letters from A to Z, underscores, and the numerals from 0 through 9. When iDVD burns the DVD, it ignores other characters, converts any lower-case letters to upper-case, and replaces spaces with underscores. If you've included some of the forbidden characters in your project name, your iDVD project name and DVD name won't match. But if you take care to follow these rules when you name your iDVD project, the DVD name always matches your iDVD project name.

Moving Your iDVD Themes

Running short of hard disk space? The themes installed with iDVD are not tiny, but they don't have to take up hard disk space if you have another disk available when you work with iDVD. You can move the iDVD themes to a location of your choosing and then let iDVD know where to find them. Also, if you purchase a themes package from a third party, such as one from iDVDThemePAK (see Chapter 17), you can tell iDVD where to find it, as well.

You can find Apple's iDVD themes in /Library/Application Support/iDVD/ Themes. Just move that folder to the location of your choosing. Then, in iDVD, choose iDVD⇨Preferences and click Advanced. The Advanced preferences contains a list of locations where iDVD looks to find themes. Click the Add button, locate the folder where you stashed your iDVD themes, and then click Open. iDVD adds the location of the folder to Look For My Themes in These Folders list. You can add the locations of third-party theme packages this way as well. Don't worry if you move the themes and forget to specify a folder location: The next time you open iDVD, it asks you to tell it where to find them.

You can use this technique to bring your themes with you if you create iDVD projects on more than one machine: Just put your themes on a portable hard disk or a network server, and then add that location to the Look for My Themes in These Folders list to the copy of iDVD that you're currently using.

Trimming a Clip Quickly

iMovie's Precision Editor is dandy for detailed clip manipulation, but you don't have to use it to fine-tune the length of a clip in your project. Press Option+⌘ when your pointer is over either end of a clip in your project and drag the orange fine-tuning control that appears to the left or right. The clip length is adjusted by single frames as you drag the control, and the number of frames added or removed from the clip is shown beside the control (see Figure 18-2).

Here's an even better idea: Put your pointer over either end of a clip and hold down Option as you press the left arrow or right arrow keys to adjust the clip's length a frame at a time.

Figure 18-2:
Taking a
little off
the top.

Doing a Slow (DVD) Burn

In a world of instant communications, microwave ovens, and other time-savings wonders, it may seem strange to want to make something go slower. However, sometimes a DVD burner has trouble with certain blank discs and fails to burn them properly at the fastest speed, but it may work perfectly if the burn speed is slower.

Although you can set the disc-burning speed whenever you start to burn a DVD, you may find doing this inconvenient if you have a 50-pack of marginal blank discs that require you to fiddle with the burning speed each and every time. In this case, you can set iDVD's default burn speed to the one that works best for you: Choose iDVD⇨Preferences, click Advanced, and then choose a speed from the Preferred DVD Burning Speed menu that appears.

Plucking Apples Off of Your Menus

Many of the themes that come with iDVD have an unobtrusive Apple logo on them. If you don't want to advertise your corporate allegiance with every DVD you make, you can hide this logo. Choose iDVD⇨Preferences, click General, and deselect the Show Apple Logo Watermark check box.

Pasting with Power

As we cover in Chapter 6, you can adjust the colors of any clip with the Video Inspector, and you can add video effects to a clip with the Clip Inspector. But what if you want to use the same adjustments and effects on several different clips in your movie?

It's a piece of cake, with rich, creamy frosting: Select the clip you've adjusted, and choose Edit⇨Copy. Next, select a different clip and choose Edit⇨Paste Adjustments, and then select an item from the submenu, such as Video or Video Effect.

You can also paste speed changes, audio adjustments, stabilization, and several other items from this power submenu. If you're a power user, take heart: There are keyboard equivalents for all the adjustments you can paste. (For example, Option+⌘+I pastes video adjustments and Option+⌘+L pastes video effects.)

Index